Psycho-Golf

Dr Willy Pasini is Professor of Psychiatry and Medical Psychology at the University of Geneva. He is the author of ten titles on psychosomatic and psychosexual medicine, which have been translated into six languages. He is also a keen golfer with a handicap of eleven. This book applies his long experience as a psychologist to the game of golf.

Psycho-Golf

Dr Willy Pasini

CollinsWillow

An Imprint of HarperCollins*Publishers*

The author would like to thank Jean Garaïalde, his golf teacher and mentor, for the instructional advice given in the book and for being the subject of the colour photography. The author is also grateful to Dr Éric Favrod-Coune for the section on golf and homeopathy and to Marie Altier for contributing to the sections on playing in competition, golf and its players, and how professionals deal with stress.

The author also acknowledges the assistance of the fifty playing professionals who contributed to the survey on stress.

First published in 1991 by
Collins Willow
an imprint of HarperCollins Publishers
London

First published in France in 1988 by
Editions Robert Laffont
© Editions Robert Laffont S.A., Paris 1988
© HarperCollins Publishers 1991 (English translation)

Cover photograph courtesy of John Stuart/The Image Bank

A CIP catalogue record for this book is available
from the British Library

ISBN 0 00 218405 2

Set in Goudy by Ace Filmsetting Ltd, Frome, Somerset
Printed and bound in Hong Kong by HarperCollins Hong Kong

Contents

Introduction

Most golf books describe the *techniques* which you need to play a shot effectively. Some also give a psychological explanation of why some techniques are preferable to others. For example Jim Flick recommends concentrating on your hands and feet because these are the parts of the body which are in contact with the ground and the club. If you use them properly, the rest of your body will naturally follow suit.

Jack Nicklaus advises using more of a vertical swing and says that the legs should play an important part in the downswing: he says this is because golf is becoming more and more of an athletic sport as courses become longer.

But most books about golfing technique remind me of cookery recipes or beauty manuals. Some of them are positively harmful because they give the impression that golf is a series of eternal truths which are attainable if only you try hard enough. But in reality, there is more than one way of skinning a cat. It does not matter which technique you use to achieve a particular objective, provided you follow the basic principles of golf: good address,

left-hand side controlling the backswing, weight shifting in the downswing, and making the entire swing a smooth, rhythmic whole.

There is also another category of golf book which places less emphasis on technique and instead describes the *strategy* of the game: how to score well in particular situations such as wind, rain or on a hilly course. These principles apply as much to the player as to the course, and you have the choice between the style of Hale Irwin, who prefers to 'seduce' the course, and Arnold Palmer, whose attitude is one of 'conquering' it!

The third category of golf book looks at the *psychology* of motivation and how it can be used to plan and play a game of golf. The bibliography at the end of this book lists a number of works by the 'Mentalists'. Charles Hogan and Dale van Dalsen were the first to use the idea of improving golf performance without dealing with the physical side of the game. In 1940, Alex Morrison emphasized the idea of visualization in his book *Better Golf Without Practice*, followed by Johnny Miller, whose book *Pure Golf* contains an excellent chapter on visualization. Bob Toski started his golf lessons with round-the-table discussions with his pupils. Jack Nicklaus's books draw considerably on the Inner Game, a concept developed recently by Timothy Gallwey.

Many professionals on the American circuit have recourse to psychologists, or at least psychological techniques. Most of them seek to attain active relaxation using relaxation techniques. Others use neurolinguistic programming (NLP), sophrology, prayer and repetition of verses from the Bible and even, in Richie Zokol's case, listening to his walkman on the course.

The aim of this book is to begin a second generation of books on the subject of psycho-golf. It is based on the following ingredients:

a. Many books are written by champion golfers who are selling their image rather than teaching golf effectively. Also, the number of psychiatrists and psychologists interested in sport, and golf in particular, is fairly small, as though golf psychology were inferior to clinical research or psychotherapy. As a professor of psychiatry who is also a passionate golf player (with a handicap of 11), I hope I will be equal to the task.

b. No-one disputes that psychology is important in golf, and that we cannot ignore the influence of the emotional right-hand side of the brain. The problem is compounded by the fact that perception and representation takes place in different ways from one person to another, and each of us has learned to perceive reality through sensations or images. You therefore need to assess how you perceive things in your day-to-day life and whether you are primarily a sensory or an image-based person, so that you can tailor your approach to psycho-golf. This book contains a number of tests which will help you answer this key question.

c. Once we have identified the main issues involved in psycho-golf, it is important to convey them using up-to-date and effective teaching methods. This book will use various strategies:

• Learning to selectively use the left-hand side of your brain (analysis and will) and the right-hand side (sense and visualization) depending on the particular golfing situation. Before the game, you will need to analyse and plan; during it, you will need to rely on your feelings as you play your shots.

• Look at your own psychology, learn to assess your own characteristics and decide whether you are a sensory or a visual person, then use this to adapt your training programme to your own needs.

• Use not only relaxation techniques, but also modern technology such as videos and computers to improve your image of yourself and your psycho-golf profile.

d. It is impossible to deny that golf is deeply rooted in the unconscious. If you can recognize its symbolic value and your complex motives for playing it, this may help you to overcome the problems you face and revive your flagging passion for golf when all seems lost.

Good luck with your psycho-golf!

WILLY PASINI

GOLF
AND YOUR MIND

In Search of the Lost Tee

• Your psychological and physical limitations

In any field of human activity, there is a combination of factors which determine whether or not you succeed. In sport, one of these factors is the difference in basic *physical aptitudes* between individuals. If you are a runner, for example, your decision on whether to take part in sprint, medium or long-distance events will depend partly on your height and weight, and partly on more complex characteristics such as your reaction times and your metabolic rate. But in addition to physical factors, there will also be sociological ones. Some cultures, including our own, encourage young people in schools, colleges and universities to become involved in sports. In other countries with different political leanings, sport is also a way of showing the superiority of a particular type of government. The successes achieved by swimmers from what used to be East Germany, and boxers from Cuba, went far beyond simple sporting competition.

There are also *technical skills* which allow you to produce the maximum performance with the minimum effort. Some sports make more use of natural gifts than technical abilities: one example is middle-distance running. Other sports, including golf, require a high degree of sophisticated technique. If we compare sports to card games, golf comes closest to bridge: if you are going to hit the ball as accurately as possible, using movements which do not come naturally to many people, you need very specific technical skills. If you ask a non-golfer to hit a ball, they will naturally tend to use the dominant right-hand side of their body, scooping the ball upwards using their right shoulder and with all their muscles tensed as though they were playing a tennis shot or throwing a beach ball. So most golf books tend to emphasize the *technique* you need to play golf strokes.

This leaves out the *psychological aspect* of playing golf, which is often mentioned in passing but rarely explored in detail. This aspect is important enough to merit the existence of an International Society for Sport Psychology in Rome, which explores:

(a) The psychological motives for playing sports;

(b) The effect that a player's state of mind has on their results, particularly in competition;

(c) The psychological consequences of playing sports;

(d) The incidental psychological benefits of sports, such as learning socialisation, self-discipline and concentration at difficult moments, controlling stress, and learning perseverance, planning and anticipation.

● Applying these principles to golf

This book deals only with the technical and psychological aspects of playing golf. However, it is worth pointing out that racial factors also play a part in people's decision to take up the game: we need only look at the small number of American professionals who are black. Sociological factors have made golf an elitist sport in the past; nowadays it has followed the example of tennis and is played by people from a much broader range of the social spectrum.

When you choose to take up a sport in the first place, and choose a particular style of play, some of the factors involved will be physical ones, such as your strength, your age and your stamina. But your limitations are not solely determined by your technique. You need only watch other people at your club, or for that matter yourself, to realize that psychological limits are often more important than physical ones. For example, if you are capable of hitting a ball straight down the middle of the fairway using a wood, but can only manage it occasionally, it is your mental attitude rather than your technique or muscular strength you should be thinking about. If you can sink long putts when practising, but keep missing when you play in competition, you probably need to listen to the message your muscles are trying to give you and decide whether psychological tension is affecting your play, perhaps without your realizing it.

There is a powerful intangible side to playing golf which can be a cause of both frustration and satisfaction, since it means you can play the same shot in the same way and achieve two different results.

In this respect, golf is not unlike hunting and fishing. All three tend to lead to emotionally charged, and sometimes exaggerated post-mortems afterwards. And in none of the three sports do you have a clearly defined objective beforehand. In fishing, you don't know whether the fish will bite or not, or whether it will be large or small. In golf, you can never predict with hundred-per-cent accuracy what the consequences of a particular stroke will be. This is where golf differs from a sport like tennis: although there are many similarities, the main difference is that in tennis a first-class player will rarely lose against a second-class one. The world tennis rankings stay more or less unchanged over the course of the year; in golf, a player simply needs to win several major tournaments in a season to become the world's top golfer.

● Playing with the right hemisphere of your brain

US PGA professional and Educational Director Gary Wiren has applied an interesting principle of modern neurophysiology to golf. We know that different psychological functions are located in different areas of the brain's left and right hemispheres. Since the fibres that transmit nerve impulses cross in the middle, the analytical, more intellectual functions of a right-handed person are situated mainly in the left hemisphere, whilst the more sensory functions are located in the right.

It is important to make full use of both sides of your brain and ensure that each takes over the leading role at the right moment. For example, if you are at an important meeting you will need to use the left-hand side of your brain beforehand, when you need to plan and anticipate what will happen during the meeting. But when it comes to the crucial moment of negotiation, if you use your intuition you will often win out over someone who has everything programmed in advance like a robot.

One example of this duality is sex. Sexual problems often happen when

the left-hand side of your brain is doing all the work. What you often need to do is stop trying to be in control and on your guard, and instead let the right-hand side of your brain take over and simply surrender yourself to the feelings and emotions of the moment.

Much the same is true of golf. In training, or during a practice round, you are more likely to be using your right hemisphere. This helps you to analyse your own strengths and weaknesses, assess the course itself and minimize the amount of risk involved. In golf, the fewer mistakes you make, the more likely you are to win. An attacking game in golf seldom wins competitions, and similarly if you run through a conscious checklist of the movements to follow, it will hinder rather than help your game. Let us look at a couple of examples:

(a) If you make a deliberate effort with the left hemisphere of your brain as you hit the ball, both your agonist and antagonist muscles will contract at the same time. This will neutralize the effect of the two groups of muscles and the swing will be shorter than if it were 'controlled' by your right hemisphere.
(b) If you begin playing golf with a checklist of ten things to remember in your pocket, you will make very little progress until you put this list in the bin where it belongs. Even thinking about two things at the same time as you swing will distract you, especially if these two things contradict each other. For example, if you remind yourself to

THE GOLFING BRAIN

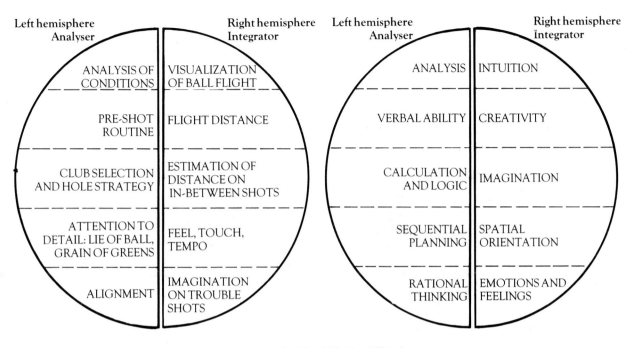

Left hemisphere Analyser	Right hemisphere Integrator
ANALYSIS OF CONDITIONS	VISUALIZATION OF BALL FLIGHT
PRE-SHOT ROUTINE	FLIGHT DISTANCE
CLUB SELECTION AND HOLE STRATEGY	ESTIMATION OF DISTANCE ON IN-BETWEEN SHOTS
ATTENTION TO DETAIL: LIE OF BALL, GRAIN OF GREENS	FEEL, TOUCH, TEMPO
ALIGNMENT	IMAGINATION ON TROUBLE SHOTS

THE BRAIN

Left hemisphere Analyser	Right hemisphere Integrator
ANALYSIS	INTUITION
VERBAL ABILITY	CREATIVITY
CALCULATION AND LOGIC	IMAGINATION
SEQUENTIAL PLANNING	SPATIAL ORIENTATION
RATIONAL THINKING	EMOTIONS AND FEELINGS

Taken from Gary Wiren's *The New Golf Mind*

make a full backswing and a long fol-. low-through, you are giving your brain a contradictory message (go back, go forward), and more often than not this will cause you to m.s-play the shot. When you play a stroke in golf, concentrate on a single priority. In the sections on practice, we show you how to focus on sensations or images rather than practical techniques.

If we accept that your mind can affect how well you play a shot in golf, the result of the game and ultimately how much pleasure you derive from it, what are the main psychological factors involved, and what effect do they have on your game?

Before you think about your own particular case, it may be useful to take a look at other people. Peter Crandford, in his book *The Winning Touch in Golf*, says that wherever possible you should learn from the experience of others; this is just as important as analysing your own technique. Ball games have existed for centuries, and our ancestors have developed and improved the movements and techniques involved. We should be able to adopt these techniques, and hopefully develop them a little further ourselves.

So it is very important to read about the basics of golf from time to time, talk about golf with your friends, go to competitions, watch golf on video,

Don't slice
Don't move your head
Don't sway

Too many things on
your mind as you
play a shot will slow
it down.

observe how others play and take lessons from a good professional. All this will be stored away and analysed by the left hemisphere of your brain, and some of it may be put to use. But things you learn may also benefit the right side of your brain. Last year, when I improved my handicap from 15 to 11, I found myself competing against players with highly co-ordinated, rhythmic and often powerful swings. By imitating them, I was able to do the same thing myself.

The learning process which takes place in golf is a smaller-scale version of what happens in life: we benefit from the body of knowledge accumulated by our contemporaries and by our ancestors. But apart from learning from things which happen outside you, the ability to look inside yourself at your own psychological aptitudes can often help you to overcome your limitations.

● Playing to win or lose

We have seen how your psychological situation can affect how you learn and play golf. Now we need to look at the opposite side of the coin and see whether golf has a beneficial effect on your psychological state. Is the golf course a place where you relax and develop yourself as a person, or is it a place where you go through every form of torture known to mankind?

Beside the golf course at Divonne in France, there is a famous casino where, fifteen years ago, I studied the psychology of gambling addiction. I found that real gamblers played to win everything, but invariably ended up losing everything. Of course there were any number of small-time gamblers who enjoyed the occasional flutter, but there were also plenty of heavy gamblers whose habit was gradually eating into their finances.

Many of these large-scale losers were people who were perfectly astute in the way they managed their money on a day-to-day basis and had obviously done well financially. But for some reason these very same people could walk into a casino and immediately lose their critical faculties. They were denying the evidence in front of their eyes: the casino had been around since long before them and would be there long after they departed this life. They were well aware that in the long term, they could only lose.

The conclusion of my research was that although they were aware of this, they unconsciously ignored it. Their desire to hit the jackpot was the excitement of attempting to break an unbreakable law; in other words, the law of the roulette wheel provided an outlet for a forbidden and unrealisable desire.

One well-known example of this syndrome was Dostoyevsky. Although he spent long periods doing nothing except losing at gambling, these periods provided the expiation he needed to restore his creativity as a writer.

To watch some people playing golf, with all the rituals, superstitions, mus-

cular tension and constant, repeated failure it involves, you could be excused for thinking that golf is simply a way of satisfying one's desire for self-punishment. If your reason for choosing golf is to restore and assert your self-confidence on a regular basis, you have chosen the wrong sport. You would be better off playing something else where you can at least get a good idea of how your strength compares to your opponent's. The technical difficulty of golf and the importance of psychological factors means that it is always unpredictable and full of unexpected events, even for top-class players.

● *Fatal attraction*

A recent film, *Fatal Attraction*, tells how what begins as a one-night stand turns to tragedy as the woman's passion turns to obsession. Golf can lead to exactly the same kind of obsession.

In psychology, we make a distinction between desire and need. Desire is the behavioural factor more common to adults, because you can activate it, control it or postpone the fulfilment of your desire. You can experience it in reality or in your imagination.

But need is part of your instincts, and can gradually take you over to the point where it becomes an all-consuming obsession. Golf should always be a desire; it should not be allowed to develop into an obsessive need. Golf has been described as the most internal of outdoor sports. It is rooted in the unconscious, where healthy and unhealthy desires are intermingled. We will explore these desires in the following section.

Golf and the Unconscious

● The psychology of motivation

Like any human activity, sport is the result of a combination of motives. Golf is both a game and a sport, and as such it is subject to more general motives which are true of any game or competition engaged in by an adult. At the same time, its technical and psychological complexity gives the game its own distinctive features, which can be divided into psychological and social motives.

If you ask people why they play golf, you will get the same contradictory answers as I received when I wrote my first book, twenty years ago. This was about the use of contraception. I asked three thousand women their reasons for wanting or not wanting a child at that particular time. The women who said they did not want a child gave very precise, and often perfectly cogent answers. But when asked why they wanted a child, their answers were often stereotyped; the most common ones I received were that they loved children and families, because it was what everyone did, and so on.

If you ask a golfer their reasons for playing, you will also get fairly trite responses. You need to go a lot deeper to discover the real, underlying motives, as opposed to pseudo-motives.

The 'healthy' reasons people give often include the need to escape from the cares of everyday life, obtaining pleasure and relaxation, closeness to nature, the aesthetic pleasure of playing a good shot, self-discipline and, of course, the desire to win.

But now take these self-same players, watch them playing on two or three separate occasions and see whether there is any clear evidence that these are their real motives for playing.

More often than not, you will be surprised by the gulf that exists between their stated motives and their latent, hidden reasons. The players themselves will probably be unaware of these, even though they may be perfectly evident to their fellow-golfers. So there is no disputing that players are motivated by unconscious as well as conscious factors. We will explore this fact more closely in the chapter on golf and fantasy, but for the time being let us look at the social or pseudo-motives for playing, since these are often the very opposite of the passionate, almost spiritual love people often profess for this sport.

• Indirect reasons for playing

Golf as a status symbol

In the same way as tennis did twenty years ago, golf is becoming less of a class-oriented game. This trend has been occurring over a considerable time, but it is still a fact that playing golf shows that you have attained a certain social level, like your car or the area where you live. Many golfers have been so successful that they have totally changed their lifestyle. Belonging to an exclusive private golf club is very much a status symbol. A couple of years ago, a friend invited me to play on a course which was surrounded by 18 houses, one for each hole of the course. My opponent gave me his visiting card, which said that he was chief executive of a large company, followed by the words 'member of the 18 club'. When I asked him why he had put this on his card, he told me that this was just as important a piece of information as his bank reference.

Snobbery

Although the situation is changing, playing golf is still in some ways an elitist activity, and membership of the right club is essential. In some clubs, members' social standing is more important than their golfing ability. The name of the club, the expensive subscription and the fact that everyone knows you belong are all features of this snobbery. Unfortunately, this seems to be an immutable fact of life.

Business

Playing golf is the ideal way of getting to know people and, ideally, doing business with them. If you play tennis with a prospective client, the two of you are separated by a net and the only time you get to meet them is in the showers or the bar afterwards. But in golf, you are pitted against them for maybe four hours, shoulder to shoulder, with all the emotions and intimacy and the intense highs and lows that golf provides. This is the kind of situation that is ideal for forging a personal, and ultimately a business relationship with your opponent. In Taiwan, the fact that you play golf is an important qualification on your cv. If you are a senior manager, you have a duty to play golf if you want to climb the career ladder. One friend of mine who gave up medicine and had an interest in finance had no trouble finding a very good job in a stockbroking company in New York. He had a handicap of 2, and the company knew that being able to provide clients with a player of his calibre to play against was much more useful than many other business skills. It was also less expensive for the company to pay for him to attend a crash course in finance than to pay for someone else to have golf lessons to improve their handicap!

Lesser of many evils

Finally, one indirect reason why

people choose golf is that they see it as an easy option. They choose it either to stave off boredom, or because they get out of breath playing more than two sets of tennis. But people who choose to play golf for negative reasons often get hooked by it, and a chance encounter becomes a fatal attraction.

● Subconscious reasons for playing golf

One of the motives for playing golf is as a means of expressing unfulfilled existential needs:

Golf as a drug

There is a well-known dictum which says: 'If you have a handicap of 24 to 18, keep an eye on your swing; if it's between 18 and 10, keep an eye on your business; if it's between 0 and 10, keep an eye on your wife.' Golf can take you over and become a drug which dominates you in exactly the same way as roulette or card games dominate a gambler. There is a difference between passion and perversion: passion is something you can control; perversion imposes itself on you and your will. To use a food-related metaphor, golf should always remain an appetite and a pleasure, not a hunger which makes you gorge on things without even noticing what they taste like.

Golf as a means of release rather than relaxation

Unlike card games, and despite the similarities between people's reasons for playing golf and playing cards, golf also provides physical exercise. At its best, it can create inner harmony and a feeling that you are in control of your own destiny. At its worst, it can also cause feelings of impulsive rage, including swearing, club-hurling and generally self-destructive behaviour.

A well-known golfing friend of mine, Jean Garaïalde, was recently playing a game with some friends. One of them had obviously got out of bed on the wrong side that day, and everything was going wrong for him; it may have been something to do with work or family problems. He was so highly strung all through the game that he was letting fly at ball, trees and grass with equal ferocity and criticizing the state of the sand in the bunkers. Eventually, his anger got the better of him, and when he got to the green at the 18th hole, he picked up his bag and hurled it into the lake in a fit of pique, right in front of a group of diners on the terrace of the restaurant. A moment later, much to everyone else's surprise, he walked into the lake, pulled out his golf bag, opened one of the pockets, took something out and threw the bag back into the water. My friend was dumbfounded, and asked him what he had in his hands. 'My car keys', he replied simply.

If you play golf for long enough, you will find that people reveal aspects of their character which they are simply unable to hide. There have been several times when I've only just managed to stop myself snapping a putter in half because I've been so angry.

Most golfers at the beginning of their careers go through a stage where their main aim is to hit the ball as hard and as far as possible. If they fail to do so, they go through alternate stages of anger, depression and even despair at their lack of golfing prowess. With a bit of luck, they will emerge from this depression unscathed and golf acquires a new significance as they realize the benefits it provides in terms of self-discipline, being at one with the environment, and trusting one's instincts. Michael Murphy's excellent book, *Golf in the Kingdom*, describes golf as part of a tradition of Scots and Oriental mythology, and gives a brilliant description of this new philosophy of golf.

Golf as a form of torture

Like many couples who develop long-term sado-masochistic relationships, many people have a love-hate relationship with golf from which it is impossible to break free. If you've reached the stage where you say: 'With a bit of luck it'll rain tomorrow and I won't have to go and play a round of golf', I think you need to reconsider whether you are still obtaining any pleasure from the game. In later chapters, we will discuss the self-punishment aspect of golf, failure-oriented behaviour and the unconscious need to lose.

Golf as a form of exhibitionism

Everyone has been through one of those situations where someone decides to show off by using their driver instead of being more cautious and playing a 3 iron. The need to flaunt your talents can upset the harmony of your unconscious and cause you to make a lot of mistakes in your swing.

Golf as a form of solitude

Unlike tennis, golf can be played alone. The complexity of the techniques involved can induce an inward-looking, repetitive attitude which some psychoanalysts have compared to masturbation.

All in all, it can sometimes be a long and hard road before golf becomes a means to pleasure rather than pain. You will need to deal with your deeper motives for playing golf and the more instinctive side of your personality if you want to avoid your unconscious preventing you from playing good golf and turn it into a valuable ally rather than an enemy. The idea behind this book is to help you reassess your unconscious, so that instead of your instinctive side being separated from your intellectual, analytical side, the two are merged into one.

● Golf is a game

Golf is a game first and foremost, a sport second. Some of the reasons for playing it will therefore be the same as for any other adult or childhood game. But there are also some characteristics which are specific to golf.

A child who does not play is likely to become sickly and depressive. Freud reminds us that playing with one's body, and then with surrounding objects, is part of a child's growing-up process. It allows the child to learn that it cannot expect immediate fulfilment of its desires every time, and to control the frustration it feels at being separated from its mother, who fulfils these desires.

Freud describes the child that plays with the bobbin its mother uses for weaving, first hiding it and feigning delight at finding it again. Freud interprets this game as an attempt by the child to use an inanimate object to control its anxiety about an animate object – its mother – since it never knows whether, and if so when, she is going to disappear from view. Using games to control the environment is an important reason for playing golf, though it is often the environment which controls the game as balls have a habit of becoming permanently lost, and therefore cause anxiety rather than pleasure!

Playing games also helps children to gain confidence through repetition. It helps them to become active rather than passive and to achieve harmony between their unconscious and the outside world. Like dreaming in adults, games can be seen more in terms of their latent content than their more overt aspects.

In adults, play often becomes a ritualized and mechanical process. Adults are not supposed to indulge in play except in specific leisure or sporting situations, where they are allowed and even encouraged to do so. Sociologists sometimes refer to this as the social control of leisure time. Nowadays, leisure is encouraged as a way of benefiting the soul, just as working twelve hours a day or more was encouraged at the beginning of this century. In those days, workers' productivity was just as important as the profitability of leisure time today.

From an educational point of view, games and sports are a place where people learn social rules and discharge their pent-up emotions in conformity with a pre-determined code. Although the American psychoanalyst Ernst Kris describes games as 'a holiday for the superego', they are rarely played for their own sake nowadays. They always needs to be justified by saying it is good for our health or useful for business.

Adults also have a psychological need for games because they allow us to interact in a more complex way than the simple, functional forms of communication that our cave-dwelling ancestors used. Culture, theatre and golf are an excellent way of expressing our instincts, so that we do not simply co-exist but can also give vent to these instincts in a way which would be unacceptable anywhere else.

When adults do not deal with and sublimate these instincts, playing games (in this case golf) can become

an outlet for persistent infantile tendencies. Another American psychoanalyst, Carl Adatto, analysed six golfers and tells the story of a patient who had such an obsessive need to play golf that he was neglecting his work. His father was a golf fanatic and had pushed him into playing golf ever since he had been a teenager, and as a result he had developed a love–hate relationship with golf. In one particularly hard-fought game, he missed a one-foot putt. He immediately gave up golf for good and became depressive because he had failed to live up to his father's expectations. It took a lengthy period of psychoanalysis before he was able to achieve a healthier relationship with golf as a game.

● Golf is also a sport

We have already noted that unlike card games or chess, golf requires a physical effort, and part of the pleasure derives from simple action.

Some of the reasons for playing golf are social ones, such as being encouraged to play it by your parents. I actually played competition tennis because my father was a good, national-standard player. My children in turn have been encouraged to take up golf as I myself did. Some clubs have whole families as members, all sharing the same passion for the game. But the children of golfers may go the opposite way and reject golf, especially if they have spent their Sundays being dragged round golf courses as caddies, ostensibly spending the day together as a family!

But apart from family reasons, it is the physical effort involved which is one of the basic motives for playing golf. Some players use it as a way of venting tensions; some find it helps them to relax and escape from the everyday world. Others enjoy the game's physical discipline and the complex pleasures of chipping and putting. Golf allows many people to develop their physical side. Initially it is physical effort and strength which are most important, with all the side-effects of muscle pain and tension that this entails. Then, when people discover that accuracy depends on how they swing the club rather than how hard they hit the ball, this creates more profound and lasting satisfactions.

Michael Murphy says that when how you feel becomes more important than how you play, it is like 'entering another world'.

Contrary to the common misconception amongst non-golfers, golf provides sufficient confrontation to satisfy the most competitive of people. It is a battle not only against your opponent, but also against yourself, a constant test of your limits in confrontation with others. Whenever you play, your physical and your mental characteristics are both essential.

● The unconscious exists

If you don't believe in the unconscious, you might as well throw this book away now. You should also ask yourself why you bought it in the first place: perhaps you had become frustrated with your lack of progress and thought it would provide rapid, cheap results, like aphrodisiacs supposedly do for sex. Or maybe you were given it by friends who were fed up with you talking about your golf problems, but were too polite to tell you and so gave you this book instead.

In reality, if we look at the unconscious outside a strictly psychoanalytical framework, the problem needs to be framed differently. It is not a case of discussing whether or not the subconscious exists, but rather to establish what practical effect it has on the other conscious motives we have referred to. Here, as elsewhere in life, there is a very thin dividing line between normal and neurotic; it is more a question of degree. Up to a certain point, anxiety can be a creative factor, but beyond this point it can become a paralyzing panic. Golf can be a very effective way of achieving self-realization and symbolically emulating other members of your family, but if you develop a need to win at any cost, your self-esteem can only suffer.

The golfing unconscious can be segregated in the same way as some classical philosophers did. In Plato's model, the mind held sway over the body. This belief was also held by the Judaeo-Christian culture, which also adopted the Stoic philosophy of striving towards a goal. This concept would be difficult to apply to golf. However, without delving too deeply into the realms of history, the hippy revolution, the green movement and the rise of feminism have all led to a reassessment of the body as a revered source of all energy, while the intellect has been stunted by a civilisation which was unable to renew it.

In golf, the aim is not to start a revolution, but simply to give the body and the unconscious their rightful importance and avoid drawing dividing lines between the mind, the will and the spirit. The 'mentalist' school of golf, which has strongly influenced this book, tries to create bridges between the mind and the body, the will and the sensations. It is in the physical unconscious that you should seek the images and sensations allowing you to perfect your swing when you despair of ever improving your game.

You should not regard your unconscious as a dangerous enemy; instead, use it and make an ally of it. It takes a long period of training, not unlike the meditation used in Christian and oriental philosophies, before you can understand your own unconscious.

Sometimes your unconscious will play nasty tricks on you and create the fantasies which make golf both a heaven and a hell.

The following chapter discusses why it is that golf is both a heaven and a hell.

• Symbolic connotations

One of the reasons why golf is enjoying increasing popularity is the rich variety of symbolic connotations which it contains. Some of these reach down to the depths of our unconscious and go back to our cavemen ancestors. Golf is a symbolic journey through the collective unconscious: like the Odyssey, it requires many sacrifices and tribulations along the way but may ultimately lead to very great satisfactions. If you are lucky enough, you will eventually experience the object of your symbolic quest: the subtle and yet all-encompassing satisfaction of golf well played, a pleasure and oneness that has been compared to that of Zen meditation.

Negative connotations

The intensity of emotion that many people put into golf, and the regressive behaviour that often occurs both on the course and at the 19th hole, are some of the negative aspects of golf. Nit-picking application of the rules, frequent disputes over trivial matters which can ruin long-standing friendships, and the frequency of cheating even by people who would not dream of doing so off the golf course, all suggest that golf brings out a predatory, even cannibalistic instinct in people. This is a reflection of the cave-dweller in all of us, and playing golf reveals this instinct in many people.

Sado-masochism

Golf is the ideal place to give vent to your sado-masochistic instincts. Fortunately, people tend to take these out on their equipment rather than on each other, by losing balls and breaking clubs. In cases like these, golf becomes an addiction which is very difficult to shake off. In really serious cases, the game can simply become an orgy of masochism.

Looking out for no. 1

I once knew a player who was nicknamed 'Turbo'. As soon as he had played his shot he would set off down the fairway as though no-one else existed. In fact, there was no room for anyone else in his self-centred vision of the world: people like this have failed to understand the real values of golf.

Religious connotations

Golf is like the road to Calvary, except that there are 9 or 18 stations along the way. The constant suffering and the alternation of success and failure are akin to death and resurrection. Golf can very easily become a Hell in which the combination of hopes, fears and disappointments the game involves seem to provide scant justification for playing it. But if you put in enough commitment, humility and hard work, and can tolerate all the depression and frustration along the way, you may be granted a glimpse of Paradise.

And what does this Paradise hold in store? According to Michael Murphy's book, *Golf in the Kingdom*, golf is a microcosm of the world, the projection of all our hopes and fears, the archetype of all games and a route towards transcendence. Golf can create a feeling of expansiveness and well-being, a feeling that you are exceeding your physical limits. Your body, your club and the moving ball are all extensions of one another. The feeling is sometimes akin to that of flying, whose exhilaration is so well described by Jonathan Livingston Seagull. Perhaps it is more than coincidence that the name of another bird, the albatross, is used to describe the very rare occasion in golf when you play a par 5 in two shots.

The glimpse of Heaven that golf sometimes provides reminds me of a story about two ageing golfers wondering whether or not they have golf courses in Heaven. They agree that when one of them dies, he will come back and tell the other whether this is the case or not.

A week later, the older man dies. He goes to Heaven and finds that it is full of wonderful golf courses. He goes back to see his friend and says: 'I've got some good news and some bad news. Which do you want first?'

'The good news', says his friend.

'The good news is that they've got lots of superb golf courses in Heaven.'

'And what's the bad news?'

'The bad news is that you've got a round booked at 9.15 on Sunday morning.'

Golf as an Odyssey

Ulysses is the prototype of modern man in quest of the ultimate truth. After his lengthy peregrinations and many brushes with disaster, he finally returns home where Penelope has been patiently waiting for him. Penelope would make a good patron saint for other halves left minding the baby whilst their spouses play golf all weekend! Ulysses' tenacity, his desire for self-affirmation and will to succeed make him a hero for the modern age; not as strong as Achilles or Hercules perhaps, but certainly more human. In many respects he is a model for golfers trying to improve their game and their handicap.

● The symbolism of golf

Playing with symbols

We live in a society which tends to value action more than it does thought, and as a result we often ignore or ridicule the symbolic significance of things that happen.

Politicians can often win elections simply by promising voters that they will take action. But in golf, this is not necessarily the best philosophy to follow, and you ignore the game's symbolic dimension at your peril. It is much better to put these images and symbols to practical use when you play than to try and suppress them. Some of them are an expression of the collective unconscious, which Jung called 'archetypes'. The green recalls the Promised Land, the blind hole is reminiscent of Christopher Columbus setting out for America without any clear idea of where it was, and an away match against another team may reawaken the Crusader instinct that lies dormant within us all.

Golf as a religion

The two oldest forms of social organization are the church and the army. There are many similarities between the church and the game of golf. Unlike many other sports which are played in noisy surroundings, golf (like religion) emphasizes quietness and contemplation. Sometimes this quietness is actually part of the rules.

The meticulous, almost ritual behaviour that takes place before a player hits the ball is very similar to the ritual of Communion. And the quasi-religious awe in which many people hold golf is very like the mystery of Christianity.

Unfortunately, religious people are often martyred for their cause, and then golf becomes more like a military campaign than a church service.

Golf and bisexuality

The way you play golf should be a fusion of male and female traits, just as we as people are a combination of male and female. To use the theory of psychological bisexuality, when you go to an art gallery and walk round looking at the pictures, you have a choice between penetrating them with your gaze, or letting them envelop you in their embrace. If you play a musical instrument, you can either penetrate the music on the printed page, or you can allow yourself to be overpowered by the music. In any situation in life, you will display behaviour that is more convex or concave, more male or female. The eye is a concave organ, but your gaze can penetrate outside objects or people. Your nose extends beyond your face, but you can use it to absorb air from outside. You can use your mouth to take in food, but also to produce sounds and words which have an effect on the outside world.

I think the same kind of principle applies to golf. Is it you that plays the shot, or does it play you? Ideally, it should be a combination of the two.

Sexual symbolism

The objects we use to play golf with have a very obvious sexual symbolism which has been the subject of many jokes. Put together a pole, two balls and a hole, and you have a symbol of sexual intercourse. But the club also has other, more profound phallic implications; it can be used as an offensive weapon or as a means of gently cajoling the ball into the hole. And female symbolism is sometimes applied to the ball: you will see a male golfer kissing a ball if he holes it, calling it a 'bitch' if it misses or saying: 'You've got to talk to the ball the way you talk to a woman'. A friend once told me he imagined his ball rising into the air like a dove of peace, and as it rose he felt himself becoming lighter. It is less common for male symbolism to be applied to the ball, except by former hunters who have turned to playing golf and liken it to a bullet.

● The symbolism of the golf course

Water

Throughout the history of humanity, water has been a symbol both of good and evil. It may take the form of a flood, which can wreak devastation or make the land fertile. It can also fall as life-giving rain. Water is a common symbol of purification in many religions. But in golf, water nearly always has negative connotations; its only use apart from keeping the course in good condition is to act as a trap for the unwary ball, even though it may be disguised with the odd plant and a couple of ducks. And rain is bad news to golfers, because it makes both your clubs and the course slippery and means you have to put on rainwear, which gets in your way. So water has largely negative connotations for golfers.

However, water also improves the visual, aesthetic appearance of the golf course. It can create that excitement that comes from fearing and desiring something simultaneously. This itself is a reflection of the contradictory feelings that golf arouses: people seek out difficult golf courses, and then complain if they don't get a good score.

Shifting sand

Much of what we have said about water also applies to sand. All of us have spent part of our childhood playing with sand, either in a sandpit or on the beach. There are relics of this symbolism in golf: if your ball seems to be endlessly trapped in the sand, you might be excused for wondering whether you are symbolically trying to revert to childhood.

And of course golf, at its worst, is a form of all-out war. It is surely more than coincidence that a patch of sand on a golf course just happens to be called a bunker.

The divot

Golfers often have an ambivalent attitude to divots. In many ways they represent an act of aggression, and for a long time my wife refused to make divots because she loved grass and thought that divots were an offence to Mother Nature. Hitting the ground with your club before you hit the ball is something you do to create backspin, but it is also a symbolic act. And replacing the divot after a shot is not simply good golfing etiquette: it is also a psychological act in which old scars are repaired and healed.

The green

The green is both the most longed-for and the most hated part of the course. It is only attainable with a great deal of effort. To some it is a fakir's bed of nails, full of hidden agonies; to others it is a garden of Eden, green and carefully tended.

The symbolism of the green is apparent in the names given to some of them. If you ever have the good fortune to play in Marrakesh, you will find that one of the holes is called Brigitte Bardot. It has two large hillocks, one on either side, with a valley running between them!

Some greens seem to have a convex symbolism to their layout, like the back of a whale whose glaring eye is represented by the hole. Others seem to have a more concave symbolism. Imagine a green set between bushes on either side, just visible in the subdued light, irresistibly evoking the mystery of the female sex . . .

The mysteries of the hole

A non-golfer might say a hole is just a hole. But golfers know this is simply not true: it may only be a little opening 4 inches in diameter, but it marks the point where hopes, fears and symbols converge. Why else is it that we say 'How many holes have you played?' and not 'How many fairways have you played?' And why is it that, like Emmenthal cheese, it is not the hole itself but what surrounds it that is important?

Holes can exert both attraction and repulsion together. If you have ever read *Alice in Wonderland*, you will know the fascination of the hole which Alice falls into, with its mysterious world of imaginary people and animals at the bottom.

If you are able to picture some kind of subterranean world beneath the green on a golf course, then you might benefit from using the symbol of the *vacuum cleaner*. If your putting lacks that certain something and you keep missing easy shots, try imagining that there is a vacuum cleaner beneath the hole sucking your ball into it.

But the hole also reminds us of the orifices of the human body, whose symbolic connotations are very familiar to psychoanalysts. Some men who are referred for counselling for sexual problems have a fear of the female vagina, unconsciously comparing it to a mouth with two rows of teeth. Advertising exploits these connotations by encouraging women to put on lipstick, and if you look at any of the photographs on a *Playboy* calendar, the chances are that the woman has her mouth half-open.

The flag

Flags have traditionally played an important part in ceremonial events. To those with an aggressive turn of mind and a penchant for westerns, the flag marks a stockade to be overrun and conquered. To others, as we have already mentioned, it has a powerful sexual symbolism.

Symbolism has both collective importance (the archetype) and individual significance. More often than not, its meaning is personal to you and no-one else knows about it, unless you refer to it in veiled form by making a joke about it, for example. But if you can recognize the symbolism of golf, you can turn it into a valuable ally rather than an enemy.

The Influence of Golf on the Mind

● The benefits of playing golf

Golf is a way of escaping the trials and tribulations of everyday life for a few hours, often in pleasant company. It helps to restore your peace of mind and helps you to rediscover the pleasures that nature has to offer.

Young people often tend to shy away from playing golf because it places more emphasis on relaxation than on venting their latent tensions and aggression. Also, good performance in golf relies more on subtle and complex muscle movements than on brute physical strength. It is a pity that they tend to view golf in this way, because it is a good way of learning to relate to others, anticipate the consequences of their actions, assess levels of risk and realize that if they stick at something, they may win through in the end. These are not always immediate satisfactions, but they are often lasting ones.

For many couples, golf is an excellent way of communicating. Lovers can often take pleasure just from being together and doing nothing, but in the long term when the initial romantic passion has worn off, love needs to share common goals and directions. As the French writer Saint-Exupery put it, 'Love is not looking at each other: it is looking in the same direction together'.

Golf is an excellent way of sharing a common interest. The handicap system means that if one partner is better than the other they can still play together without too many problems, unlike tennis where if players are unequally matched the less experienced player can end up tired and demoralized.

Marriage guidance counsellors say that if two people want to live together despite the apparent lack of similarity between them, then they must have at least some objectives in common. Even having shared enemies can be good for a couple. For example, if you have over-dominant parents who threaten to drive a wedge between you by being over-protective about their offspring, the act of forming a united front against them can actually bring you closer as a couple. The practical difficulties of playing golf represent both a positive goal and a joint adversary to be overcome.

Alternatively, you may be single, at the peak of your powers and successful in your career. But it is all too easy to be severely stressed by events around you and forget that quality of life is more important than money. In cases like these, golf can often be an excellent reminder that your lifestyle needs changing. It shouldn't take a heart attack to realize that the quality of your life is not as good as it might be. Golf is a good way of compromising between work and leisure, helping you to make more free time for yourself and achieve a more balanced existence.

Several of my colleagues in the medical professions are also tennis partners of mine. They tend to arrive at the changing rooms running, with their last patient's file under their arm. They talk shop while they change, get the game and the showers over as quickly as possible and then disappear straight back to work. In cases like these, sport has actually become a part of their stressful lifestyle, and the likelihood of its having any physical or mental benefit is very small.

Golf, however, takes time to play. Because you play it in an attractive outdoor environment, it is a much better way of taking your mind off things, especially since it requires a psychological as well as a physical effort, which can be a powerful distraction from problems at work. When I tee off from

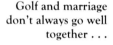

Golf and marriage don't always go well together . . .

the first hole at Divonne, I have to cross a symbolic stream to reach the second hole. This increases the feeling that I am crossing a kind of frontier and escaping from the outside world.

For older people who love golf and regard it as an essential part of a balanced existence, golf has the benefit of taking longer than many other sports. Some people end up in an early grave because they do not adapt their sporting involvement to their physical ability as they grew older. There are still any number of 65-year-olds who will emerge exhausted and bruised after a 40-minute game of tennis and take nearly two hours to recover. This takes them up until lunchtime, and because they are retired it means they face an afternoon with nothing to do! Golf is very popular amongst older people, partly because it offers opportunities to do business but also because it allows them to share an activity with someone else for several hours.

But it is easy to over-emphasize the potential benefits of golf. All of us know a young person who puts all their pent-up explosive energies into golf and gains no benefit by playing it. For couples, golf can perpetuate conflict-based, sado-masochistic relationships. Many people who are highly successful and therefore narcissistic in other areas of life find it hard to cope with failure in golf. Elderly people sometimes have an embittered attitude to life and use golf to take their revenge on others. This also helps to explain the extraor-dinarily high frequency of cheating amongst golf players who are otherwise very honest in their day-to-day lives.

● The true satisfactions of golf

There is a great deal of pride involved in being able to drive the ball a long way, or being able to use a shorter iron than another player to hit the ball the same distance. But the real psychological satisfaction of golf goes deeper than this: it is the pleasure of being master of yourself and your environment, the expansion of your self-image and your skills.

Being in command

Psychologically, golf should be a half-way point between total control and total relaxation. If you try to exert too much control over a situation or a movement, you are likely to overload the analytical right-hand side of your brain and your muscles will not be sufficiently relaxed. If you are too relaxed, there is a danger of being distracted; your grip will be weak and your swing will not be incisive enough. Sometimes, feigning relaxation can conceal a lack of assertiveness and energy which psychiatrists associate with latent depression.

Being in command means being sensitive to the situation and in a state of active relaxation. To use a comparison with sex – since it is an analogy familiar to most people – if you try too hard and have excessively high expectations, this can cause problems with erection and/or orgasm. And if you are too relaxed, you are likely to be asleep before your other half has finished! If you can acquire this half-way stage between control and relaxation, which we will call 'being in command', your confidence and personal satisfaction will increase, not only on the golf course but also in your everyday life.

Expanding your personal space

A well-played shot gives a pleasant feeling of harmony with the club, the ball and the world around you. Sometimes you will feel as though your own personal space has expanded, as though things around you have become an extension of your body. This feeling is often experienced by archers, whom the American psychologist Michael Murphy has compared to golfers. A good archer is one who feels that the arrow is a part of themselves and their movements, and see this movement as an extension of their own physical limits. Other sports players describe their sports in similar ways. Alain Prost, the motor-racing driver, who is also a good golfer, told me he found it much easier to judge high-speed turns if he imagined the car as an extension of himself. Bernard Russi, the skier (again, also a golfer), told me he saw his skis as an extension of the soles of his feet and 'felt' the snow through his boots.

We live in a stressful society which places a heavy psychological burden on us, and this feeling of well-being and self-expansion is a rare one. It is sometimes encountered in some of the finer moments of sex, or when creating a work of art. Golf can help make those rare moments of existence a little less rare.

The feeling of dexterity

In 1987, I played a cup competition in Crans with someone I had not partnered before. His swing was not perfect, but he had a very effective technique on and around the green, with a light touch that characterized all his chips and putts. I myself had hit 13 greens in regulation, only to three-putt five times, and I watched this man's skill with a certain amount of envy. During the game, I found out that he was a very well-known plastic surgeon. I would unhesitatingly recommend him to any of my clients and would even go to him myself if I had to: his dexterity with a golf club gave me every confidence in his skill with a scalpel!

• The negative effects of golf

Psychosomatic problems in golf

We all have our own different ways of reacting to stressful situations in life, depending on our psychological makeup and the experience we have acquired as we have grown up. For example, Hilde Bruch studied obese children and found that when they used crying to express their unhappiness as very young children, their mothers would give them either the breast or the bottle to calm them, though the main effect of this was to appease their mothers. This habit of using physical means to satisfy psychological needs may continue into adulthood: for example, a massive eating and/or drinking binge at the 19th hole after a bad game. But more often, unresolved conflicts originating on or off the golf course can be manifested in other parts of your body. Whether it consists of insomnia, migraine, stomach aches or cramp caused by too much muscle tension, these are functional symptoms which often affect golfers under stress and may be an alternative to actually expressing the underlying unhappiness. The survey of professional golfers and their reactions to stress at the end of this book shows just how common these symptoms are.

Various studies in the psychology of competition have shown how champion players are able to control their emotions but tend to regress into psychosomatic symptoms when they are unable to achieve the high level of performance they seek.

Physical problems like these can also occur in good golfers who are being slowed by age or overwork. Because of lack of time or muscular skills, they are no longer able to play to their handicap. They will often go through a stage of nervous problems and unhappiness, or even deep depression concealed by psychosomatic symptoms, before they can admit the truth to themselves and start enjoying golf for its own sake.

Another, less common form of psychosomatic disorder is hysterical conversion. A child with a stomach ache may find that this can provide additional benefits in terms of attention from their parents. They may therefore be tempted to feign symptoms at difficult times in life to make people worry about them or to deal with overstressful situations. These are known as 'hysterical conversion symptoms', and they have wrongly been regarded as solely a female preserve. The symptoms are less common in the golfing world for the simple reason that hysterical personalities tend to be incompatible with the psychological requirements of golf and tend to choose other sports where quick decision-making and speed are more important than tenacity and constant hard work. A hysterical personality that needs an audience is more likely to do well in a game like tennis, whilst a golfer has to keep up the same level of performance for four hours or more. So psychosomatic symptoms in golfers are likely to occur in obsessional, meticulous personalities with analytical, rather than instinctive tendencies. Because the left-hand side of their brain is doing all the work, they are likely to suffer from physical tension.

Anger, depression and masochism

Unlikely though it might seem, anger and depression are two sides of the same coin. If you do not express your anger properly to the outside world, it will be repressed and directed against yourself instead. This is an act of self-aggression, which we call 'depression'.

We have already discussed the difference between explosion and expansion, and the benefits of being assertive rather than violently aggressive. If you are trying to bash the living daylights out of the ball when you drive it, you are unlikely to hit it as far as you might. Anger, like anxiety, is very harmful in golf, though it does have the advantage of being more short-lived than anxiety, since it usually turns fairly soon into resignation or even depression.

I sometimes play with a very good friend of mine who suffers from severe muscle tension, reflected in his stiff set-up and the way his jaw and left forearm muscles contract almost in spasm. When he is like this, I am always careful not to stand in front of him, because there is a very high risk of the ball going in completely the wrong direction. I have never seen him in this state for a whole four hours because it gradually turns into depression and pessimism. All this can lead to failure-

It's all very well being a perfectionist, but you can risk being penalized for slow play.

oriented, self-destructive behaviour: it is almost as though the player has decided that since they cannot excel themselves by playing well, they might as well excel themselves by playing badly instead. This attitude is familiar to psychologists, who find that in any group situation there will always be someone who is unable to act as a positive leader and prefers being a negative leader to being a wallflower.

Peter Crandford, in his book *The Winning Touch in Golf*, advises against being masochistic when playing golf. Strange though it might seem, just as some golfers go all out to win, so others have an unconscious desire to lose. Some players seem to be plagued by constant misfortune, simply because they have an unconscious need to punish themselves. Some are happy just to get round the course; others have a reputation for being good losers.

Like fear and anxiety, depression may be a reaction to the events – in this case failure at golf – which cause it. At other times, failure can reflect a more deep-seated worry about the whole purpose of life.

Even some championship players are essentially pessimistic and use missed shots as an excuse to feel sorry for themselves. Of course there is bad luck in golf, just as there is good luck, but what distinguishes one player from another is how they deal with it. What often happens is that people are overcome by anxiety and tension during the game and depression sets in afterwards, because the results obtained are rarely those expected.

Although this is what normally happens, depression can also be used positively, like fear; both can have an adaptive function. Looking at artistic creativity, for example, we find that very few people write music when they are feeling happy with their lives; Liszt and Rossini are exceptions. Many composers express themselves best when they are in a state of unhappiness or even despair.

Depression may be the first step towards increased awareness of your situation, which in turn prepares you for the process of change. If you don't get depressed or self-critical sometimes, there is no chance of your changing, on the golf course or anywhere else!

There are various remedies for depression: some are pharmaceutical, some psychotherapeutic and some physical.

I. Unlike narcotics and anxiety-reducing drugs, anti- depressants are less often abused by sports players. These are only likely to be used as part of proper medical treatment by a doctor. If possible, choose a doctor who plays golf or other sports, since this will reduce the risk that he or she will prescribe anti-depressants too readily!

II. If your golfing problems are caused by failure-oriented behaviour and more general lack of confidence, psychotherapy may be a good idea.

III. More recently, the physical approach has shown a great deal of promise. It may involve an assessment of your posture, stance, gestures and voice. Professor Klaus Scherrer has studied the voices of people suffering from depression and found that their voices lose intensity and become more high-pitched. A series of vocal exercises has been developed, using body-mind techniques to reduce levels of depression. The psychologist Daniel Casriel has worked with drug addicts and the controversial American psychiatrist, Arthur Ianov, has experimented with severely disordered people using screaming therapy.

It is also possible to work on physical posture and gestures using body-mind techniques, since the way you express yourself bodily can often affect your state of mind. In the past, the emphasis has been placed more on mind-body techniques, where your state of mind can affect your body's reactions. If you look at the posture of a depressive person, their lack of energy will often be manifested by walking with a stoop and with their stomachs sticking out. People like this tend to keep their gaze fixed on the ground and look as though they are bearing the woes of the world on their shoulders.

One way of treating a person like this is to tell them to jump up and down, wave their arms around and shout 'I'm depressed!'. Their physical behaviour will often overcome their state of mind because it is physically impossible to be depressed if you are skipping and throwing your arms around. Try it for yourself!

Likewise, if you are anxious, this can often be reflected in the way you present yourself to the outside world: your voice may be harsh and tight, your facial expression taut, your jaw clenched, your brow furrowed and your gestures rapid and jerky.

There is a lot to be learned from looking at people's postures. Look at an anxious golfer setting up for a shot, and the chances are you will see three typical anxiety symptoms:

a. They duck their heads as though protecting themselves from danger;

b. They breathe poorly, taking deep gulps of air;

c. They shift the energy in their body upwards in what is known as 'grounding'.

If you think you might fit any of the above descriptions, try imagining that you are a giraffe, eating leaves from the top of a tall tree and thereby making your head independent of your shoulders. If this does not work, try lumbering along like an elephant to make your feet more heavy, or imagine yourself with roots coming out of the soles of your shoes instead of studs.

Unfortunately, golfers who are not in command of their emotions are often those who are least likely to accept that they may be displaying psychosomatic symptoms when they play golf.

It is rare for golfing problems to be

If you are feeling tense at address you will have a tendency to hunch your shoulders, which makes it difficult to turn them. To help relax, imagine you are a giraffe munching leaves from the top of a tree.

so bad as to need psychotherapy, but if you do experience psychological problems which come to the surface when you play golf, you should take a psy-chological approach to solving them. So golf is not just a sport; it can also provide valuable psychological insights if you choose to use it that way.

It is better to be poised and confident than slouching and depressed when you address the ball.

The Influence of the Mind on Golf

In the previous chapter, we looked at some of the psychological traits which result from playing golf. In reality, many of these exist before you start playing and may affect how you play it.

We will now look at what happens if you have too little or too much confidence, if you are afraid of winning or of losing, if you suffer from anxiety and mental tension, or if you indulge in risk-seeking behaviour. First of all, though, we will look at some of the physical and mental principles underlying the game of golf.

● Physical and mental principles

Your body is a combination of different parts. As well as serving a physical function, these parts also have a psychological role when you play golf. What we are interested in here is how the different parts of your body interact with one another and the environment, and in particular the way in which you perceive your own body.

Imagine your body as an onion, with many concentric layers. The top layer is your skin, which serves as a sensory organ. Underneath this are your muscles, which provide movement. The next layer is your skeleton, which gives you balance and stability. Finally, the fourth layer contains your internal organs including your brain, which is the seat of your emotions. Each of these four layers plays a greater or lesser part in how you play golf.

a. Your sense of feeling

We sometimes describe a good golfer as having a 'feel' for the ball, or say they have golf in their blood. How you feel when you play golf is important. Feeling the ball through the head of your club, being able to sense the difference between different lofts and the flexibility of the shaft (stiff or regular) are all examples of the highly developed sense of feeling which characterizes top-class players.

Underneath your skin is the fine musculature, which is responsible for the more delicate, complex movements of golf. The ability to make these movements is easy to lose if you have been out of practice for a long period of time.

b. Muscles and motor functions

This is one of the subjects described

most often in sports psychology. Whilst a physical sense impression can be distorted by the way in which your imagination perceives it, there is a much more direct connection between the motor functions and your physical actions. Your muscular makeup, and whether you are short and stocky or tall and thin, will affect both your performance and your muscular metabolism. The muscle fatigue that builds up as you exercise sometimes does more harm than mental fatigue in a golf tournament that goes on for four days.

Your state of mind can play a very considerable part in your muscular makeup. It can have a positive effect, by stepping up the metabolic rate of your muscles when you need to concentrate during a match. It can also have adverse effects by making your muscles too tense and therefore wasteful of energy. In other sports, such as diving, this loss is tangible and measurable. A beginner who is anxious, and therefore breathing too heavily, uses up to 50 per cent more compressed air than someone breathing normally.

Something of the same thing happens in golf, though it is less easy to quantify. All golfers have experienced a situation where they have played a tournament and ended up exhausted afterwards, even though they have not exerted themselves any more than the other players. This is because the others are more mentally or physically relaxed and therefore use up less energy.

We know that the muscles have their own reflex 'memory' which allows them to learn from previous experience and is primarily linked with the right hemisphere of your brain. This is why it is beneficial to practise strokes on your own, especially more subtle approach shots which need more complex handling of the ball. But don't go on mechanically practising shots for hours, because this will increase your anxiety level and do more harm than good.

It is important to exercise this muscular memory when you are training and practising, though you should realize that you will not always obtain immediate results. A good training strategy involves carrying out an exercise with a specific objective, but the results will not be visible until several days later when your muscular memory has taken them on board.

Don't underestimate the importance of conscious willpower, but give it its proper place in your golfing strategy: use it when planning, not when playing. When I was a child, I was encouraged to study using the example of the Italian writer Vittorio Alfieri, who had himself tied to a chair at his desk so that he could get on with his work without being distracted. His motto was 'volli, sempre volli, fortissimamente volli': 'willpower, always willpower, strong, strong willpower'. I don't think Vittorio Alfieri would have made a very good golfer.

Willpower should come into its

own when you plan training sessions, but not during them when your motivation starts running out and you get bored with repeating the same action over and over again.

c. The skeleton and your stability

The structure of your muscles is based around a combination of articulated bones and tendons. Some of these come under considerable strain when you play golf. As you grow older, the articulation of your muscles becomes less flexible, and this means you cannot rotate your body so far during your backswing. Your skeleton also provides support, balance and stability: it is the framework around which the rest of your body moves. Good articulation and mobility are essential in golf, though too much articulation increases the risk that your swing will turn out different every time. You should also try to avoid stretched muscles dominating your skeleton and causing cramped, constricted movements. This is particularly important at the end of the swing. Pietro Manca, the doyen of Italian golf professionals, told my wife to end her swing 'proudly, not like a little old lady'. The aim is to finish the movement facing the target, with your hands well up in the air.

• Lack of confidence

If you feel self-confident, you are likely to play better golf. You cannot be both self-confident and anxious at the same time, and fear is the worst thing that can happen to your swing. It tends to activate the wrong muscles and prevents the right ones being used. Part of your confidence comes from the way you are playing golf at any given moment, and part of it comes from your underlying confidence in yourself and your personality which exists independently of golf.

This confidence is difficult to acquire, because it involves overcoming both technical and psychological problems at the same time. You will not be able to get the ball near the flag

A smooth and relaxed swing will end with a strong follow-through and leave your hands high.

43

very often if your approach technique is wrong, but equally it is possible to be very familiar with the technique but too tense to perform it properly.

It takes a great deal of experience and practice to improve – or acquire – this confidence. We hope this book will help you to do so. Peter Crandford describes how Paul Runyan once told Mac Murphy, former president of the US PGA, that when he had improved his short game to the point when he knew he could get down in two shots, his long irons and woods became much more accurate. Because he was no longer dominated by the fear of missing the green with his approach shot, this removed the psychological shortcomings in his long game.

In golf, confidence is the result of good technique, hard work (if possible with a good pro), repeating your successes and choosing attainable goals. Most golfers tend to ignore the evidence of their ability as evidenced by their handicap. If you have a handicap of 12, you need to remember that on the six most difficult holes of the course you have only a 50 per cent chance of making par. You should therefore minimize the degree of risk involved and maintain a level of confidence which matches your abilities. But if you try to obtain the best result on the most difficult hole on the course, you may already be stretched by a performance above your abilities. This tension will make it hard to play the shot well, and undermine your self-confidence on later holes.

Many people tend to say: 'The 10th is an unlucky hole for me: I haven't been able to hit the green with my first approach shot for six months', or 'I always have trouble with the 13th'. This is a vicious circle, where poor strategy leads to too much tension, which causes increasing self-doubt and lack of confidence, which means you keep making the same mistakes.

Golf is very good at bringing out certain aspects of people's characters: one of these aspects in particular is lack of confidence. I have a friend who plays long iron shots very well and vents his anxiety by hitting the ball hard. However, he often has problems with his short game, where lack of confidence in himself and his abilities makes him concentrate on his strokes too much and he spends too long in the set-up. This leads to constant mishits.

Because golf requires such a high level of technical and psychological abilities, anxiety is often linked to previous times in your life where lack of confidence has led to failure, perhaps at school, at work or in a relationship. Lack of confidence can occur at any stage in your development as a person. For example, one of the most common causes of failure is the memory of sexual failure. Golf is often seen as a test of virility for men – and for some women as well.

But failure in golf can also be caused by the very opposite: fear of success. We have already discussed how the fear of failure can actually lead to failure: now we will look at the other side of the coin.

● Fear of success

Some people have been brought up in the belief that success is a natural consequence of hard work, or even a reward for it. But others have come to believe that it is a sin to succeed, for example in competition with their same-sex parent or their brothers and sisters. It is almost as though the very fact of succeeding means that others must fail. Unconsciously, they believe that only one person can be successful at a time, in golf or anywhere else. If they become that successful person, then they must have done so by depriving someone else. In psychological terms, people like this have a problem with the idea of object deprivation. For example, if a child has a toy and gives it to another child, they are deprived of it themselves. This causes them a dilemma. But if you have a piece of technical knowledge which you can share with someone else, that other person will be enriched without your becoming any the poorer. In this way, the act of sharing enriches both parties.

If you have still not overcome these vestiges of infant behaviour, you may be afraid of winning because it means taking this success away from someone else and therefore exposing yourself to possible reprisals.

There are many other motives for the fear of success, but they are beyond the scope of this book. They are often the reason why some people break up when they come under stress when playing golf. For example, it is not uncommon for someone to play really well for seventeen holes, realize that they may win the match and register a double bogey at the 18th to lose.

Lack of confidence can also be caused by lack of motivation, or conflicting motives for playing golf. If you play golf not for enjoyment but to keep up with the Joneses, or because your husband or wife plays golf and you don't want to be left at home holding the baby, the pleasure you get from the game will be limited and your self-confidence poor. If any one of your motives for playing golf is excessively dominant, there is a risk that it will undermine your performance and sap your confidence.

● Over-confidence

If you are over-confident, this will inevitably have an adverse effect on your game. If you are a good player and things are going your way, every good game you play will boost your confidence and help you to achieve consistent results. But if you are less of a good player, winning a game or tournament having played better than your handicap may create the false belief that you can repeat the same success the following day. This over-confidence may lead you to spend too much time resting on your laurels at the 19th hole, which will make your success that much harder to repeat the next day. You will find you are less tolerant of your own mistakes, and ashamed at feeling so proud of yourself the previous day. If your expectations are unrealistically high, you will be irritated at your inability to achieve them. As the pendulum swings back the other way, you will lose confidence.

In other sports such as tennis, an attacking game may pay dividends in the way that it does not in golf. The kind of play that wins a game of tennis will lose a game of golf.

Also, with the exception of a few champion players, over-confidence is simply not compatible with a game that lasts for four hours or more and involves dealing with so many technical and psychological problems.

So although positive thinking is essential in golf, you should always tailor it to your own abilities. If you adopt a moderately critical attitude to your play during and after a game, you should be able to see yourself in a positive light without getting so conceited that it ruins the next game you play.

• Anxiety and fear

No matter whether you are a beginner or a world-class player, differing degrees of anxiety play an important part in your game. We have already mentioned fear of failure and fear of winning, but there is also the fear of your self-image being dented if you are placed at the bottom of the league table in the clubhouse.

But because golf requires complex mental and technical skills, you will always suffer from some degree of fear, or at least anxiety. Of course some golfers deny that it exists, but this does not mean they are immune to it. One of my patients was suffering from high blood pressure, but he was so convinced that there was nothing wrong with him that it took a severe attack of dizziness and a fainting fit before he would accept that he had a potentially serious health problem. I have had other patients sit in front of me at my desk and swear that they are perfectly cool, calm and collected, and yet their foreheads are covered in perspiration.

This disparity between people's perceptions of themselves and their actual situation is particularly common in golf, but less easy to measure. An awareness of this disparity is often what distinguishes good golfers from bad ones.

Audiovisual methods, particularly the use of mirrors and video cameras, are particularly beneficial in golf, since they can highlight emotional and physical symptoms of which you would otherwise be unaware. All of us experience tension, whether we like it or not: the important thing is to be aware of it and turn it to our advantage.

Tension is part of the alarm syndrome described by the psychologist Hans Selye in his book, *The Stress of Life*. Fear is conveyed by neurotransmitters and causes adrenalin to be released. Ultimately, fear serves a positive function: an antelope which does not experience fear is likely to be the first to get eaten by a lion. So fear puts you on guard against danger, and in golf a reasonable amount of fear will stand you in good stead because it will make you more able to determine the proper strategy to follow. But fear can get out of control if you over-react to the source of danger; in other words, when your fears are more imaginary than real. If you get anxious when you go near a water hazard because you lost a ball there on a previous occasion, your emotional reaction is not a fear that it *might* happen again, but a belief that it *will* happen again.

If you are obsessed with negative experiences in the past, your fears are likely to get out of control. They may be expressed in a whole variety of psychosomatic symptoms: muscular tension, palpitations, shallow breathing, stomach aches and even insomnia on the night before an important match. On the course itself, a very common symptom is playing one shot badly and then rushing the next one so that things get even worse. In some ways, mis-hitting shots is a good way of working off excess fear, and it is often the cause of those disastrous holes which could have reasonably been salvaged with just a bogey.

On the green itself, fear can mean that you hit your first putt and then hit another one straight away before it is your turn to play. When this happens, there is the danger that the second putt

will miss as well. Experienced players use a series of rituals, such as cleaning the ball, replacing it and breathing slowly as they do so, to prevent them from hurrying a shot through fear.

A good swing in golf creates a feeling of expansion in you, making you feel that the limits of your personal space extend to the end of your club and into the ball as it flies through the air. But fear and anxiety can turn this expansion into *explosion* in which you release all your energies simultaneously rather than co-ordinating them into a harmonious movement with a clearly defined beginning and end.

There are many different antidotes to fear and anxiety. Some of them are specific to golf; others are more generalized.

I. Learning to have more confidence in your technique is a reliable tranquillizer. So regular lessons with a professional are even more important in golf than they are in other sports.

II. Drugs may seem to provide a miracle cure for anxiety, but this effect is short-lived. You may well feel relaxed if you drink a bottle of champagne before the game, but this relaxation is not going to last for the entire duration of the game.

Opinions differ about the use of anxiety-reducing drugs, including tranquillizers. From a neurological and physiological point of view, benzodiazepines and especially beta-blockers slow down the exchange of information between neurons and the rest of the peripheral nervous system. This can make it difficult to carry out and synchronize the complex movements that golf involves. Other tranquillizers, such as valium, have a dual effect on both the central and peripheral nervous systems. Valium is also a muscle relaxant, which can work in your favour, since nearly all golf players suffer from stiff muscles. So the muscular benefits of medicines like these have to be weighed up against their adverse neurological effect.

Amphetamines can improve performance in other sports such as tennis, cycling and athletics, but they do not appear to have any significant benefits for golfers. Amphetamines make you less tired, but they also make you highly strung, as you will know if you have ever used them for slimming purposes. This more than outweighs the advantages they provide in terms of faster reactions. If you use mild sleeping drugs (not barbiturates) the night before a tournament, they will give you a good night's relaxing sleep, which outweighs the slightly toxic effect of the drug. Another good thing to try is a sports massage after the game, or alternatively a long hot bath which will relax your muscles and dilate your blood vessels to increase the flow of blood.

III. It is also worth pointing out that anxiety can be caused by problems which differ very widely in importance.

For example, you may be very laidback in your day-to-day life, and yet be a bag of nerves in major competitions. Alternatively, you may normally suffer from anxiety verging on phobia or neurosis, and yet shed this anxiety when you concentrate on playing golf. Finally, anxiety can be caused by a more basic lack of confidence, and a weak ego. This may need psychotherapy, but the result is bound to have a favourable effect on your golfing performance.

IV. If you are less interested in the reasons why you are tense when you play golf, there are many other forms of therapy available which try to control anxiety rather than understand why it occurs. They include hypnotism, meditation, the various forms of relaxation (autogenic training, Jacobson's relaxation), yoga, transcendental meditation and biofeedback. Some of these techniques are described in the following chapter.

● Enjoying taking risks

How much we enjoy risk or fear varies from one culture to another and from one individual to another. The self-made businessman or woman who succeeds by taking risks tends to have high social status in many Western societies. In a more rurally-based society, with fewer organizational structures, people need to take risks if they are to achieve any form of social advancement. In other societies, the risk of losing is regarded as being more important than the risk of winning, and people prefer not to take chances.

In golf, the latter attitude is the one which is most likely to stand you in good stead, except in specific situations such as match or team play. Golf is an excellent way of learning to take calculated risks and tailoring the amount of risk you take to the nature of the course and to your own golfing ability. Jack Nicklaus often says in his books that amateurs he has played with in Pro-Am tournaments tend to take much greater risks than he does, such as choosing a 3 wood to get through a clump of trees or pitching their approach shots instead of rolling them.

Any golf player faces this equation between risk and benefit. But as in poker, you can only take risks and outbluff your opponents if you have a good hand of cards. In golf, you can take more risks if you have a well-developed technique; paradoxically, it is often the very opposite which happens. Taking risks may bring you short-term benefits, but just because you have won a battle does not mean you are going to win the war.

● In conclusion

There are often psychological factors underlying golfing performance, but conversely successes and failures in golf can cause intense emotional reactions: this is a kind of circular process. I think it is true to say that the psycho-logical side of the game is more than 50 per cent responsible for the final result. But it is no good simply being aware of this: you also need strategies which will help to improve the quality of your game. This was my main reason for writing a book on psycho-golf, which casts a critical eye at the 'mentalist' schools of golf and develops a psychology which is particular to golf.

Having psychological problems is not very fashionable; nor is the idea of going to talk to someone about them. People who go to psychotherapists often do so under the pretext of a particular disorder or symptom, such as bulimia, headaches, the menopause, or a specific sexual problem. I actually teach dental psychology as part of the psychology of medicine, and I have had referred quite a large number of child psychiatric cases by orthodontists. Children who need braces for their teeth often start to display regressive behaviour because they have to give up sucking their thumbs, which they use to provide psychological reassurance. A brace can also be the solution to many difficult psychological problems which would be hard to treat in any other context. There are strong grounds for believing that golf is an opportunity to deal with anxiety, depression or psychosomatic symptoms experienced in everyday life. The three examples below show how beneficial this can be.

1. In other sports, such as football and skiing, the psychologist plays as important a role as the coach and forms an

integral part of the team. Swiss skiers have improved their performance in downhill events by using relaxation techniques in which they have learned to suppress their fear and approach the slopes with even greater determination.

2. In football, psychologists used to be a luxury; now they are becoming a necessity. They have already helped many top players to improve their performance.

3. When I was working in a psychiatric hospital in New York, I knew a psychologist who was also a long-distance runner and treated his patients whilst running round Central Park. Because the patient was relaxed and sharing an activity with the psychologist, it was easier to deal with difficult problems than sitting at a desk or lying on the psychoanalyst's couch.

The profession of golfing psychologist has still not gained widespread acceptance in Europe. You need only look at what goes on at the 19th hole to realize that it would provide a full-time job for a psychologist! There are countless self-obsessed golfers looking for a sympathetic ear to listen to their latest golfing mishaps, and a dire shortage of people willing to listen. So many post-match conversations are monologues. Developing the study of 'psycho-golf' may be the first step towards making psychotherapy standard practice in golf.

Strategies for Problem Golfers

● How and why

Why

Many golf magazines have a section on the psychology of the game. They will advise you to play golf by minimizing the amount of risk you take in relation to your ability, play in a positive and confident frame of mind, and remember that it is a game and not a life-or-death battle. Sometimes articles of this kind will give you practical advice for reducing stress or restoring your confidence by concentrating more and knowing how to relax. Often, they will suggest that you increase your visual acuity by staring at the ball or, alternatively, close your eyes to concentrate on your feelings. Many of the more recent books have placed the emphasis on how to reduce stress; this book is more concerned with telling you why you should do so.

In the previous chapters, we have seen that at its best golf is a passion; at worst it is an obsession and a form of torture. Like all passions, it is rooted in the enigmatic and fascinating world of the unconscious. People's reasons for playing range from the very obvious to those they would be unwilling to admit or discuss with anyone else. It is often the latter which account for the strange way some people start to behave as soon as they walk onto a golf course.

I once played in a charity tournament with a very good club player who had a handicap of 5. During the game, he never stopped complaining about his poor swing, though there was nothing wrong with it that I could see.

On the 17th hole, he played a perfect shot which took his team into the lead. When his partners congratulated him, he grumbled: 'Well, anyway, my set-up was really atrocious!'.

This player was a perfectionist, but he was misusing his skills and using golf as an excuse for self-chastisement. He went on being pessimistic, even when events proved him wrong. Players like this are unlikely to obtain any relaxation from the game. If we were to improve his handicap (though not his enjoyment of the game), we would need to delve a little deeper into *why* he was behaving like this.

Having a low handicap is not necessarily the key to happiness. On the contrary, many top-ranking golfers are in a constant state of torment and have a truly sado-masochistic relationship with golf; Sunday players who can't hit the ball in a straight line are often a great deal happier.

If you want golf to be a passion without turning it into an obsession, it is useful at least to have an idea of why you prefer it to other forms of leisure-time activity. It is much easier to go to someone for advice about a golfing problem than about a psychological difficulty. I know several golfers suffering from chronic stress who would baulk at the idea of consulting a psychologist or a psychiatrist, but don't think twice about having relaxation treatment to help reduce their handicap!

How

In a problem marriage, we can analyze why the couple argue, why they chose each other in the first place or, if the worst comes to the worst, why they still stay together when they cannot stand the sight of each other. If we can find out why they have problems, then they can receive therapy which tells them how they can deal with these problems. We can suggest how they can find other ways of using up the energy which they expend in having rows, or how to communicate better if they find it hard to change their personalities. Ultimately, we can tell them how to find the positive side which exists even in a crisis.

Much the same applies to golf. Teaching golf should be a combination of 'why' and 'how': exploring the deeper reasons why you play golf in the first place, and how you can use mental and physical exercises to help you play better.

We will discuss this process in more detail in the chapter on learning. The purpose of this chapter is simply to describe some of the best-known relaxation techniques. We will not be looking at psychotherapy, hypnosis, behavioural techniques or humanist psychology, because all of these require the help of a therapist. There are plenty of other books which will tell you how to go about finding therapy.

● Relaxation techniques

It is difficult to give a clear definition of the concept of relaxation techniques. There are many different techniques which use mental and/or physical exercises to change the way your muscles and your emotions behave.

It is important to make the distinction between passive forms of exercise which you undergo, such as various forms of physiotherapy and massage, and those which require your active participation. Active exercise requires you to learn how to make your own mental and physical changes.

Schultz's autogenic training

This method dates back to the beginning of this century. It was inspired by the works of Vogt, who asked subjects about their physical experiences during hypnosis. Most of them made some reference to feelings of heaviness and warmth. Schultz invented a series of self-training (autogenic) exercises to change physical feelings through thought. He described the following experiment, originally devised in 1826.

Sit down squarely at a table and hold a pendulum made of a piece of string about a foot long, with a heavy object on the end, between the ends of your two index fingers. Now, if you imagine the pendulum moving, it will start to do so. If you place a watch underneath the pendulum and move your eyes across the face of the watch from 6 o'clock to 12 o'clock, the pendulum will start swinging, apparently of its own accord, in the same direction. If you now make the same movement deliberately, you will get a completely different feeling of being keyed up and tense.

In other words, if you think of something happening and concentrate on it, this will set up an involuntary, but perceptible movement in your muscles. For example, if you want to relax your arm muscles, all you need to do is concentrate your mind on the relaxed state you are trying to achieve. The act of relaxing will be reflected in a feeling of heaviness.

If you are tense when playing golf, try sitting in an armchair with the back of your neck supported by a cushion, your arms resting on your thighs and your palms downwards. Close your eyes to help you concentrate and think the following thoughts, as intensely as possible but without moving or speaking:

• I am completely calm
• My right arm (or left arm if you are left-handed) is very heavy.

Repeat this exercise for one to two minutes, two or three times a day. Breaking the process up in this way is more beneficial than a more sustained period of relaxation. Then gradually extend the feeling of heaviness to other groups of muscles. This takes practice, because if you actively try to relax it will only make you more tense. You will also need to overcome your fear of being passive and not being in control. It is also important that, if you are feeling stressed, you make the time for the exercise and believe in it during the first few days when you are unlikely to get any tangible results.

This may well involve reorganizing your lifestyle to allow for a few minutes' pause during a busy day when you feel out of control. For this reason, the first few sessions normally take place with a therapist, who will help you to question your own values, your quality of life and your priorities.

Autogenic training involves six exercises, the first of which we have already described.

1. Weight exercise (muscular relaxation): my body feels heavy.
2. Heat exercise (vascular dilation): my body feels warm.
3. Controlling your heartbeat: my heart is beating calmly and strongly.
4. Breathing control: I am breathing calmly.
5. Controlling your abdominal organs: my solar plexus feels warm.
6. Head exercise: my forehead is cool.

After each session, you should go

through a cooling-down period to end the exercises. The usual sequence advised is this:

- Flex and extend your muscles several times;
- Breathe in deeply;
- Open your eyes.

This treatment takes two to four months, and involves one session a week with a therapist, lasting about 20 minutes.

Schultz's technique is of proven effectiveness, although some therapists have said that his ideas are over-simplistic. Many patients are sceptical during the first session, but as time goes on they are amazed by the changes they find taking place in their bodies. The use of simple, repeated phrases in Schultz's autogenic training is similar to that of mantras in transcendental meditation. This repetition, reinforced by the method's suggestive effect, is a very good way of altering your level of awareness and restoring neural functions which have been adversely affected by stress.

Jacobson's relaxation

Edmund Jacobson's method uses progressive contraction and relaxation of the muscles. It involves learning the different states of muscle tone and the perception of movement.

The treatment requires an hour a day, alternating with sessions with the therapist over a period of one year. Unlike autogenic training, which involves concentrating on different physical states such as heaviness and warmth, but not moving, Jacobson's relaxation requires you to actively contract and relax your muscles. A typical session would take place with you sitting in a comfortable armchair, with your arms and legs uncrossed, and listening to the therapist's voice, either in person or on tape. The therapist says:

'Relax as much as possible and listen to me counting down from 10 to 0, with a pause in between each. I am going to show you how to contract specific muscles and analyse the feelings you experience. First of all, clench your right fist as tight as possible but keep all your other muscles relaxed. After 20 or 30 seconds, your fist and arm will start to shake. Concentrate on your muscles and what you feel when they are stretched. Now open your hand and relax, let the tension flow out of your arm and feel the sensations as your muscles become relaxed.

'Now, clench both fists as tightly as you can, and again concentrate on the feeling of tension, then let go and feel what it is like to relax.

'Push the palms of your hands together in front of you so that your biceps contract. Keep doing this until your arms are tired, and feel the contrast between the contracted muscles and the relaxed ones.

'Cross your two index fingers and pull outwards so that your shoulder muscles contract. Then put your arms along the arms of the chair and see how heavy they feel. Enjoy the pleasure of the tension going away.'

This relaxation process is gradually extended to the whole of your body, using specific exercises for your face, neck, chest, abdomen, thighs and lower limbs until the whole of your body is relaxed. This helps to find out which parts of your body are most often tense so that you can concentrate on them in the exercises.

Some principles of Jacobson's technique anticipate the approach of increasing the tension until it goes away, rather than trying to get rid of it voluntarily. Golf teachers also use this technique by telling pupils to deliberately exaggerate the mistakes they make most often.

Muscular tension is assessed based either on the patient's own subjective impressions, or by the therapist feeling the muscles, or using biofeedback.

Wolpe's systematic desensitization

This American therapist began by modifying Jacobson's technique and then developed his own method, combining the benefits of relaxation techniques and mental images. If you are suffering from stress and go to see a therapist who uses this method, he or she will ask you to make a list of the stressful situations you encounter in your life, ranging from the very minor ones to those you have major problems dealing with. These might include imagining yourself teeing off in front of a large audience, getting past a water hazard, or sinking a downhill putt.

At the first session, you will be asked to tell the therapist about the first situation you have listed and at the same time carry out physical relaxation exercises. By a process of elimination, known as body–mind, when your mind and your body are working at cross purposes, it will often be your body that wins the struggle. The process of physically relaxing reduces the amount of anxiety linked to the situation you are thinking about. After this you will go on to the next problem situation, but not until the first objective has been attained.

Desensitization usually begins in the therapist's consulting room, but later on you will gradually do more at home and use the technique in real-life situations. The therapist may even go onto the golf course with you to carry out the therapy. This technique has been successfully used to treat a wide variety of phobias and is often used to combat fear of flying.

● Biofeedback (BFB)

Biofeedback uses electronic equipment to detect, amplify and reproduce physiological and psychological reactions which are normally inaccessible to you because they are unconscious, involuntary and automatic.

In the laboratory, it has proved possible to change the alpha and theta brainwaves, blood pressure, heartbeat, muscular tension, salivation and sexual response to name but a few. The best-known application of this technique is in lie detectors, which identify abnormal responses to each question. Your body is constantly making use of its own 'instrumentation' to analyse your body's reactions to things you do (biofeedback) and make adjustments if necessary. For example, if you are playing sports and have used up most of your available energy supply, biofeedback creates the sensation of hunger. Sometimes these stimuli are subconscious, and sometimes you are so stressed that you are no longer aware of your physical and mental condition. In this situation, it can be useful to make use of biofeedback instrumentation. This includes:

• The electromyogram (EMG), which displays the electrical potential of your muscles on a screen. The electrode can be fixed to the muscles on your forehead or any other part of your body. You then use a combination of concentration, relaxation, breathing, mental images or any other useful method to reduce your score as shown on the screen.

• The electroencephalogram (EEG), which measures the amplitude and frequency of your brain waves. When it was found that yogis produce a higher number of alpha waves (waves of 8–10 cycles per second), scientists tried to reproduce these waves in people who needed to relax. As soon as the EEG shows an alpha wave, the subject is given feedback in the form of sounds and has to try to reproduce this feedback by attaining the same state of relaxation again. This technique has been particularly successful in the United States, where it has been used on thousands of people. This is another form of therapy which you might try as a golfer.

• Galvanic Skin Response (GSR) measures the galvanic reflex of your skin, whose electrical resistance changes as your emotional state changes. The skin's electrical reaction is caused by the sweat glands innervated by the sympathetic autonomous nervous system. Any anxiety reaction can therefore be detected via the skin.

• Other instruments can be used to measure the temperature of your skin, your blood pressure, your heartbeat and your sexual reactions before they become visible to the eye.

The principles of biofeedback have already been widely used in golf. Another valuable analytical tool used is the video, which has largely taken over from the use of the mirror. Here, the feedback is provided in the form of a video of your swing, and this is used to produce a biological reaction in the form of an improvement. Scientists can also analyse the plane of your swing and the way you transfer your weight, using computers attached to sensors placed beneath the floor.

Biofeedback has been used in fields as varied as teaching musical instruments, rehabilitating accident victims, and treating a variety of psychosomatic symptoms such as headaches and high blood pressure. Its value to golf has long been underestimated, and it has many other potential uses:

• Helping people with poor self-awareness who do not know they are stressed to become more aware of their condition. Here, biofeedback is essentially being used as a form of lie detector for golfers.

• Making the player more aware of the particular situations which make them anxious when playing golf, by wiring them up to biofeedback equipment so that when they think of those situations, they receive quantifiable feedback.

• Improvements while learning can be monitored using BFB. For example, if you are learning deep abdominal breathing to make you more relaxed, your progress can be recorded electronically. BFB can also help you to realize the powerful effect that anxiety can have on your performance.

For example, if you are being hampered by the fear of playing a hook or a slice, here are some possible antidotes:
• Concentrate on the idea that your mind is completely empty and no harmful thoughts can get in.

• Consciously realize that the thought is there, and then consciously rid your mind of it.
• Breathe out gently and imagine that the obsessive thought is moving down your body and out through your feet.
• Imagine the cool, clear water of a mountain stream refreshing and cleansing your mind.
• Imagine destroying the thought with a flamethrower.
• Imagine your mind as a blackboard and then rub out the harmful thoughts.

The BFB control will indicate which image will suit you best. You are now ready to start thinking positively.

• The Feldenkrais method

Moshe Feldenkrais was born in Russia, and worked in France for a long period before emigrating to Israel, where he recently died. His method is based on analysing posture and movement. Feldenkrais believed that we had lost our kinetic awareness as the species evolved and we therefore express ourselves clumsily in our everyday lives. We need to free our nervous system and physical behaviour from the bad habits we have acquired. He believed that it is easier to change our bodies than our minds, and therefore developed a form of mental physiotherapy. His techniques are used in a large number of centres all over the world.

For example, he developed an exercise to free the nape of the neck, which is so often blocked in golfers trying to achieve good shoulder rotation. Very often, you will find you are so conscious of how you ought to be doing something that you end up breathing shallowly and hunching your shoulders. This makes it impossible to rotate your shoulders consistently. Feldenkrais's exercise is as follows:

1. Sit down comfortably and turn your head to the left and right, without making any effort. Work out how much of the surrounding space you can see.
2. Move your right arm over your head and touch your left ear with your right hand. Do the same with your left hand and your right ear.
3. Repeat the same exercise, but this time follow the movement with your eyes, as though your gaze is an extension of the rotation of your neck.
4. Now do the same thing again, but as you rotate your neck outwards, turn your eyes in the opposite direction, in other words towards your nose.
5. At the end of this experiment, relax and look at the visual space you can reach by rotating your head to the right and left. In general, your mobility will increase so that simply by rotating your head without moving your shoulders, you can obtain 360-degree vision.

To free up a movement which has become stiff, Feldenkrais uses a process of neurological deprogramming, by sending contradictory messages to the analytical centre of the brain. It is not usual to touch your right ear with your left hand; nor is it usual to turn your neck but not move your eyes at the same time.

● Sophrology

Definition
Sophrology is a discipline which studies (*logos*) the harmony (*sos*) of the mind (*phren*). It was pioneered by a Spanish-born Colombian doctor, Alfonso Caycedo, and its success is due in large part to the fact that it can be practised without the aid of a therapist, at least at basic level. Sophrology uses a variety of methods including breathing and visualization to attain a level of reduced alertness, half-way between wakefulness and sleep, known as sophroliminal relaxation.

These relaxation techniques draw fairly widely on exercises from other Western approaches such as hypnosis, autogenic training and Jacobson's relaxation, and Eastern philosophies including yoga, Buddhism and Zen.

Static techniques
Start with a short initial period thinking about the tensions you suffer from as a golfer, and begin to relax your mind. Then loosen your muscles using techniques from Jacobson's relaxation.

The next stage is called *simple sophronization*. Sit in a comfortable position, breathe deeply and close your eyes. Then think about the different parts of your body one by one, in as much detail as possible. This will gradually help you to relax physically.

Next, relax your mind. One way of doing this and achieving reduced awareness is to keep your eyes closed and look downwards and inwards towards your nose, as though crossing your eyes. If you exhale deeply and repeatedly, you will gradually move into a state of deep relaxation.

Alternatively, move your eyes upwards. Whichever you do, this process should take about ten minutes in all, and will take you to the *sophroliminal level*, which forms the basis for everything else that you do. Like other relaxation and hypnosis techniques, at the end of the whole exercise you should consolidate what you have done by breathing deeply, shaking your hands, feet and head and finally opening your eyes. The following two techniques may help you deal with golf-induced stress:

Progressive sophro-acceptance

Once you have achieved physical and mental relaxation and reached a state of sophronization, you could try some active and positive visualization. Imagine a situation occurring in the future, perhaps in a couple of months' time. Make it a realistic one, not something that is total fantasy: one example might be receiving an award at a prizegiving ceremony. Imagine the place, the time, and the people and objects present in as much detail as possible and try to see yourself growing into this situation. This will help you to see the future in a new and more optimistic light. As you continue with the exercise, gradually bring the positive image forwards in time until eventually it is tomorrow, the day of your competition.

Synchronous sophro-respiration

Once you have reached the sophroliminal level, say a word with pleasant connotations to yourself, such as 'par', every time you breathe out. Gradually replace this with another word from deeper inside yourself, such as 'birdie'.

One way of increasing the value of this exercise is to use a method called sophroliminal protection. If you have trouble getting to sleep before a match (which, according to the survey at the end of this book, is a problem afflicting 30 per cent of professionals), try saying the word and at the same time visualizing a future situation, such as going to bed. Later on, at bedtime, this will help you to transfer this state of sophronization to the bedroom and help you sleep.

Dynamic techniques

Dynamic sophronization includes various Oriental techniques which Dr Caycedo learned from his wife.

• Step 1: *Concentrated dynamic relaxation* (inspired by yoga). Begin this technique standing up and end it sitting down. Once you have reached a state of simple sophronization, breathe in as deeply as you possibly can, lift your hands up to your face and block your nose with your thumbs. Then breathe out and bring your arms down again. Repeat this first exercise three times, then do the next exercise, which is the same but with your eyes and ears blocked. Finally, do the third exercise, which involves making head and neck movements and breathing freely at the same time. Concentrate on the way your different muscles feel, and end the session relaxed and lying down. There are also other exercises for the rest of your body.

• Step 2: *Contemplative dynamic relaxation* (derived from Buddhism). Begin in the same way, relaxing first your muscles, then your mind and finally your breathing until you reach the sophroliminal stage. Then contemplate the different parts of your body and stroke them as you do so. Start standing up and move into a sitting position, concentrating on the parts that feel most tense; you might also try focusing on your five senses as well as your body.

• Step 3: *Meditative dynamic relaxation* (based on Japanese Zen). Sit in the upright position, with your back away from the back of the chair. Clench one hand and place it on your stomach, then put your other hand over it, open. Concentrate on deep breathing, synchronized with the pressure of your hands. Half-close your eyes and stare at

the ground. Do this meditation in complete silence: you could also try walking with your steps in time with your breathing. Gradually, you will find you attain a greater inner harmony.

Despite this deliberate use of Eastern techniques, sophrology is firmly based on Western principles:
• It uses your perception of your body as a way of tapping into your vital energy;
• Positive actions always have positive results, a very useful concept in golf where stress affects everyone at some time;
• Sophrological methods are very firmly rooted in objective reality. In other words, when you practise sophrology you do it as a golfer, not as a Buddhist monk.

• Homeopathy and golf

At first sight, there might not appear to be any connection between homeopathy and the psychology of golf; in fact it almost seems a contradiction in terms to talk about using medicines in a game that involves relaxation, concentration and being at one with yourself. But homeopathic medicines can provide a valuable adjunct to other methods of combating stress and tension such as those described above.

In many respects, medicines offer a temporary solution to these problems, and as soon as the medicine wears off they start to recur. You can cure the symptoms, but you can't necessarily cure the underlying causes. Golfers are all too aware of this fact: the questionnaire at the end of this book shows that only 25 per cent of golfers questioned used medicinal aids of any kind, and even they tended to use the mildest ones possible. It is possible that even this figure is slightly overstated if you think that the definition of 'medicines' could also include a swift half or a cigarette before the match.

In many ways, medicines are a last resort, an emergency measure, an admission of failure, an acknowledgement that you cannot perform at your best without some kind of outside help. A problem golfer in a panic at the prospect of an audience watching their every move in a Pro-Am tournament, or totally dependent on a particularly good score, may well benefit from being calmed by a carefully chosen medicine. But you can be sure that a really top-flight champion will have no need for that kind of thing.

So why use homeopathy? There are at least two reasons, the most obvious (but not necessarily the most correct) being the absence of side-effects. A well-chosen, properly diluted homeopathic remedy is not going to transform you from a bundle of nerves into a zombie staggering from one green to the next. The other reason is that there is an enormous range of homeopathic medicines to choose from, so there is a very high chance of finding one that suits you. The converse of this, however, is that choosing the right one can be difficult.

Homeopathy treats by similarities: if you give a sick person the right homeopathic remedy, it will relieve or even cure the disorder provided it is able to create the same symptoms as the disorder if administered in large quantities to a healthy person. In other words, for a homeopathic remedy to be effective you need to analyse your symptoms, then choose the remedy which creates symptoms the closest to your own. This is not an easy task, and is beyond the scope of this book.

There are plenty of books on homeopathy designed for the layperson; better still, go and see a homeopathic doctor. Often you will find that if you don't succeed first time round, you will need to try something different; but there is a strong likelihood that eventually you will find the right remedy for your particular problem.

The following is a list of some of the main remedies and their principal symptoms. These are the symptoms which they cause if given in large doses, and therefore which they may cure or relieve in very small doses.

Gelsemium

This is the best remedy for nerves. The general symptoms it may relieve include feelings of weakness, depression, a heavy head, headaches and

neck and shoulder tension. It may also help if you have problems swallowing, especially hot things, or feel you have a lump in your throat.

Another of the essential symptoms of Gelsemium is stress-induced diarrhoea of the type that causes you more inconvenience than discomfort. It may help your breathing if you feel as though there is a weight on your chest. Likewise, it may be good for your heart if you have a slow pulse and the feeling that your heart is about to stop beating, or if your heart races every time you make the slightest movement. Gelsemium can also be a cure for insomnia caused by excitement on the night before an important match.

Ignatia

This remedy has some points in common with Gelsemium. It is largely a remedy for emotional disorders including nervousness, apprehension, rigidity and trembling. The symptoms may be superficial and change frequently; they may include a heavy or hollow-headed feeling, and your face and lips may twitch. If you have a hollow feeling in your stomach and find yourself burping all the time, Ignatia may be the answer; likewise if you suffer from stomach cramps, a rumbling stomach or involuntary movements of your fingers and toes.

Baptisia

The main symptoms helped by this remedy are extreme weakness and fatigue, inability to think, depression, inability to swallow anything but liquids, lack of appetite, diarrhoea, pains in the right-hand side of your stomach and a suffocating or breathless feeling.

Ipeca

Ipeca is a remedy for many symptoms which may affect you as a golfer, principal among which are persistent nausea, irritability, and painful, watery eyes. The nausea may be accompanied by constant salivation. The symptoms may include difficulty in inhaling, a tight chest and coughing every time you breathe in.

Aconitum

This is the best remedy for anxiety: not the minor nerves that affect any golfer at the tee-off, but major anxiety and panic attacks, uncontrollable physical and mental agitation. These are the kind of symptoms which hit you suddenly, not gradually. Essentially, Aconitum is a remedy for fear: fear of the future, fear of crowds, crossing the road, fear of anything and everything. But it will also relieve other symptoms including heavy-headedness, headaches, dizziness when you wake up, hypersensitivity to noise, dry mouth, dry, furry tongue, a dry, burning throat which makes anything except water taste bitter, intense thirst, colic and breathlessness. But essentially, Aconitum is a treatment for the kind of fear and anxiety whose symptoms suddenly appear from out of the blue.

Belladonna

This is another of the most widely-used homeopathic remedies and can relieve a considerable variety of symptoms. Unlike Aconitum, it is not a remedy for extreme thirst or anxiety, but again it is best used for symptoms which appear suddenly and unexpectedly. These include extreme excitability verging on anger or even rage, and hypersensitivity affecting all your senses (hearing, sight, touch, taste). You may feel hot, with a red, flushed face, or you may have a dry mouth and throat but not actually feel thirsty.

One symptom of auditory hypersensitivity is the impression that your own voice is ringing loudly in your ears: if this happens to you, belladonna may be the answer!

Other symptoms which it is likely to help include lack of appetite, a swollen stomach, violent palpitations whenever you make the slightest effort, and the feeling that your fingers and toes are cold even though your skin is flushed, hot and dry.

Magnesia phosphorica

This is a remedy for disorders where the emotional element (nerves, fear, anxiety) is less important and physical symptoms, particularly cramp, muscular spasms and the pain that goes with them, are predominant.

It is particularly suitable if you feel tired and worn-out, if your body hurts all over and you get a headache whenever you try to make any mental effort, or if you feel cold all the time. You may have colic and wind which get better if you go into the warm or relieve the pressure on your stomach, perhaps by loosening your clothes. In many ways, the symptoms most typical of Magnesia phosphorica are muscular ones: palpitations and chest pains, twitches, cramps, muscle contractions and spasms, and general weakness in your extremities. It is excellent for depression, fatigue, and lack of physical and mental energy.

Psychological symptoms where Magnesia phosphorica is indicated include anxiety, weariness, irritability and listlessness. You may feel unwell, but not physically sick. Your back, leg and arm muscles may feel extremely weak, especially after exercise. The important thing about all these symptoms is that they get worse if you are worried or anxious or if you make any kind of physical effort.

Colocynthis

This is also a remedy for the kind of stomach pains and migraines which occur when you are irritable or jumpy and get annoyed when people distract you. These stomach pains are often severe, brought on by the slightest problem, and can only be relieved by putting pressure on them. Colocynthis is also useful for muscle spasms and hip and knee pains.

Silicea

This is another remedy for people who are nervous, anxious, excitable, hypersensitive or unusually sensitive to cold. Your forehead, neck, feet, hands and armpits may sweat more than usual, and the perspiration is often cold. You may also suffer from cramps and tremors in your hands and elsewhere every time you try to use them.

Coffea

This may be useful if you are suffering from irritability, agitation, excitability or violent headaches which are made worse by noise. It is also good if you have an unusually large appetite, insomnia, violent palpitations or an irregular heartbeat.

Coffea can be an excellent remedy if you want to relax before an important round of golf.

Strammonium

Most of the symptoms for which this is suited are mental ones: excitability, agitation, excessive cheerfulness, and an inability to stop talking, fidgeting and making jokes, sometimes in rather bad taste. This cheerfulness quickly turns into sadness, though this is equally short-lived. Another symptom associated with this remedy is unusual feelings in your body: feeling that your arms and legs are separate from the rest of your body, or that certain parts of your body have become fatter than usual. But the main symptom is excitability, a constant need to be talking, laughing and doing things and an inability to cope with being on your own.

Some homeopathic remedies are so wide-ranging and relieve such a large number of symptoms that they are almost certain to do you some good as a golfer suffering from stress. Some of these are as follows.

Natrium muriaticum

Hypersensitivity, fear, lack of enthusiasm, headaches, paleness, nausea and eye problems, stomach aches, sweats whenever you eat anything, cravings for salt, sharp pains in your chest, palpitations, an unusually powerful heartbeat, sweaty, clammy palms, weak, flabby arms and legs: all of these symptoms may be relieved by this remedy.

Nitricum acidum

Symptoms include irritability, belligerence, aggression, pessimism, extreme hunger, stomach pains which are relieved slightly if you tighten your belt, and athlete's foot.

Nux vomica

This remedy is for you if you are nervous, hyperactive, stressed and pressured but lead a sedentary life. Other symptoms include a constant need for coffee or other stimulants, and eating and drinking in large quantities, more out of need than pleasure. This kind of temperament makes you unpredictable, ill-humoured and hypersensitive. Nux vomica is also good for nausea and flatulence after meals, constipation, and feelings of bloatedness and weakness in your extremities. The symptoms are likely to be at their worst in the morning, after you have undergone particular psychological strain, or when you have overdone the eating and drinking.

Sepia

Sepia is indicated if you feel heavy, weak, cold (even in hot weather), indifferent, sad, solitary, sensitive and unpredictable. Other common symptoms are dizziness, headaches centred on your forehead, breathing problems, palpitations, muscle tension, aches and pains. It is also useful for those times when you find yourself fidgeting uncontrollably.

Arsenicum album

Like many other homeopathic remedies, this is a well-known and powerful poison, but when diluted for homeopathic purposes it has many different therapeutic benefits, particularly for the nerves, the mind and the muscles. Its symptoms include a feeling of total exhaustion any time you do anything, combined with a feeling of irritability; extreme and unquenchable thirst, fear, fright, worry, cold sweats, depression, and lack of courage and energy. Your stomach may churn at the very idea of food, and you arms and legs may be afflicted by shaking, cramps and weakness.

Aurum

This is the remedy for those times when you feel extremely pessimistic, depressed, useless, hopeless and aimless; in extreme cases, it can be used by people who are feeling suicidal. However, it is also effective against excessive hunger and thirst, and against an irregular heartbeat which sometimes seems to stop for two or three seconds at a time. The feeling of blood rushing to your head is very common, especially if you feel unwanted and depressed at the same time.

The seventeen homeopathic remedies described above are, inevitably, a small and arbitrary cross-section of the many hundreds which are available. Any of them could be appropriate to your specific case. Equally, you may feel that your symptoms do not match any of those described above: this is quite normal, and it is unlikely that they will match exactly. So start by analysing your symptoms, and write them down if necessary. Then choose the remedy which seems closest to your own situation. Buy a tube of the remedy in granular form, diluted to 7 to 9 CH (Centesimals Hahnemann, the unit of dilution). Dissolve four to five granules on your tongue as soon as you feel the first symptoms. You can safely repeat this dose one to two hours later if the first does not appear to have any effect. But if your second attempt doesn't work, don't keep trying: you simply need to try a different remedy.

TEACHING GOLF:
THE THEORY AND
PRACTICE OF LEARNING

How to Teach

This section of the book will look at teaching golf from the coach's point of view, whilst the following chapter will look at the learning process from the learner's point of view.

Golf teaching is based on the same general principles as any other form of teaching, with particular emphasis on the psychology of sport. There are four essential requirements for a good teacher:

1. Knowing the technique to be taught,

2. Being familiar with the educational and psychological principles that will enable you to transmit this knowledge,

3. Being able to assess your pupil's personality,

4. Being positively motivated to teach.

We will not be examining the technical knowledge that is transmitted, since we assume that you will have acquired this as part of the process of qualifying as a golf coach. What we do intend to explore are the psychological aspects of teaching, with the emphasis on what you should and should not do.

DON'TS

● Contradictory messages

I have lost count of the number of times I have heard people who are not qualified as teachers telling other people to relax. This gratuitous and unasked-for instruction is often given by one member of a pair to the other in a friendly game, or by one member of a married couple to the other, or by a parent to their offpsring. Even some professional coaches give out messages like these, simply because the pro is unaware of the different functions performed by the right and left sides of the brain.

Telling someone to make a conscious effort to relax is a contradiction in terms. All it will do is make them even less relaxed! The closest analogy is with insomnia, where the harder you try to get to sleep, the harder it is to do so.

One characteristic of a good teacher is their ability to teach techniques which achieve the results sought by indirect methods. For example a good way of dealing with a pupil with tense forearms is to point out how their right knee should move in the downswing. This will stop them thinking about their arms and relax their muscles.

Another way of approaching this problem is to ask the pupil to make their arms as tight as possible: this will get rid of the tension simply because after a while their arms will be exhausted!

• Teaching negative ideas

The same message can be expressed in two different ways, positive and negative. In golf, as in life, your brain is often better able to deal with a positive instruction than a negative one. 'Keep your head still' is likely to be more effective than 'Don't move your head'. Likewise, if you tell a pupil to keep their weight balanced you will probably get better results than if you tell them not to sway.

• Too much in one go

Because learning golf is a complex process, there is a temptation to squeeze as many ideas as possible into a single lesson. When I first started playing golf, the pro teaching me used to pack at least ten different instructions into each session. Although there was nothing wrong with the way he explained them, you should avoid overloading pupils with too much

information which is correct in terms of technique but not in terms of educational psychology.

Other pros give their pupils one exercise to do at a time, without telling them the indirect aim which they are trying to achieve. This requires a certain amount of commitment by the pupil towards the teacher and a willingness to undergo coaching for a sustained period of time, but it can be very beneficial for some players.

To use a food-related metaphor, if you eat a good but large meal, there is a danger of confusing hunger with appetite and over-eating as a result. In psychotherapy, the amounts of speaking and silence need to be carefully balanced so that thoughts and ideas have time to sink in. In golf, it is better to break your teaching up into manageable quantities than to overload your pupils with instructions.

• Creating excessive dependence

This brings us to the relationship between pupil and coach. Apart from relatively neutral situations, such as a short course of lessons while on holiday, it is common for an emotional bond to be created: this may be anything from a positive alliance to outright hostility. Sometimes, the pupil may become psychologically dependent on you as their thirst for knowledge conflicts with the frustrations involved in learning golf. In cases like this, they may well come and see you three times a week, just as people get used to going and lying on their psychiatrist's couch three times a week. The risk of your pupil becoming too dependent is increased if you obtain narcissistic satisfaction from this dependence.

When I worked for the World Health Organisation, I found the same problem existed as far as developing countries were concerned. We had the choice between sending them boxes of dried fish or teaching people how to improve their fishing techniques. Although the latter took longer and was more complicated, in the longer term it was more likely to help countries become independent of outside aid.

game gets worse in the short term. In other cases, where the pupil is less motivated, less physically agile or not such a fast learner, you may need to narrow your horizons and work on what they have already learned. What is most important is that this choice should be based not on your own personality, but on your pupil's abilities. If you use a single method for every pupil you may be successful with some of them, but in others you may find they drift away from you. But it can also be bad for a pupil if you are too flexible and willing to adapt your style to theirs.

Psychologists face this kind of problem every day: do we help our patients live with their problems, or do we try to work on the underlying causes?

● Radical change or partial modification of the swing?

This is the main dilemma which faces all teachers of golf or, for that matter, any other sport. If you are a pro working in a holiday resort, you will have only short-term contact with your pupils and will therefore have to adapt to their playing style. But if you have regular contact with them, it can be hard to decide which type of teaching to use. Sometimes (especially with younger and more highly motivated pupils) you will need to be drastic and tell your pupil to make radical changes to their style, even if it means that their

● Boredom and lack of motivation

Some golf teachers love teaching and will tell you that it increases their own enjoyment of the game. Other pros teach because they are not sufficiently successful on the professional circuit to earn a living solely from playing golf. So ask yourself, on a regular basis, how motivated you are to teach. Otherwise, disenchantment and boredom will set in and eventually your teaching will be a waste of time. If you do not enjoy your job, and think your talents could be better used elsewhere, then you are unlikely to fire your pupils with enthusiasm for golf.

DO'S

• Identify the problem

As we pointed out in the previous chapter, there is no single technique which works for everyone. So teaching always needs to be tailored to the particular golfing problem that needs to be solved: this problem may be one of technique, or it may be psychological, or a combination of the two. For example, if your pupil's forearms are too stiff, you should ask yourself whether this is simply a fault in their technique or whether they have a more deep-seated psychological block.

• Concave and convex attitudes

Doctors generally fit into one of two psychological categories. Some are warm, maternal figures who are good listeners even if there is a queue of people waiting to see them. Others tend to be more strict about the amount of time they spend with you, and dispense prescriptions as a symbol of their authority. I call the first category 'concave', and the second 'convex'. Over the years, if you are a doctor competing with other doctors in your area, you will achieve a kind of balance between your own personality and what your customers want. Some patients want a warm, welcoming, concave doctor and will go out of their way to see one; others prefer the more authoritarian type of doctor who tells them very firmly what to do.

Much the same division exists amongst golf pros, and each category will tend to get on best with a certain kind of pupil. Ideally, you should be able to switch between the two depending on the type of pupil and the kind of things you need to teach them.

• Tailoring your teaching style

This suggests that an open training programme centred on your pupil's aptitudes rather than your personality is likely to be more successful. In medicine, the phenomenon of compliance is well known: if a patient is prescribed medicine but is not convinced it is working, there is a 20 to 30 per cent chance that they will stop taking it. The same applies to diets. At other times we see the opposite problem: patients believe that medicines (especially injections) will provide a miracle cure, when really what they should be doing is changing their lifestyle.

In golf there is the same gap between the theoretical value and the practical effectiveness of teaching. This is why it is a good idea to check now and then that what you have said has actually been taken in, perhaps by a quick question-and-answer session at the end of the lesson. You may be depressed by the results, but they will improve the quality of your teaching.

• Group teaching

Apart from the fact that group teaching is more financially rewarding than individual lessons, it is often more beneficial to the pupils. My family find it easier to remember things they have been taught in golf clinics than in individual lessons. Group teaching is often particularly effective with young people because they are so good at imitating others. Although there are some specific golfing problems where one-to-one teaching is a better idea, group coaching tends to be more successful.

There is plenty of evidence for this in other areas of medicine. One example is ante-natal classes; another is Weight Watchers, where people wanting to lose weight motivate each other by giving rewards and penalties for successes and failures. Psychotherapy aimed at helping people to give up smoking is also more likely to be successful if carried out in a group.

• Mnemonics

We have already seen how it is better to teach using positive rather than negative terms. It is also important to teach mnemonics to remind pupils of important points to remember when they go out onto the golf course. I have always told medical students that there should be three Ts in the relationship between doctor and patient: time, tact and talent.

a. The golfer's equivalent of the doctor's three Ts could be PRO: posture, route, and objective. This mnemonic contains three essential things to think about before you play any shot: the posture you adopt at address, the route you want the ball to follow and the objective you want to attain.

b. A simple mnemonic for an anxious beginner playing a chip shot might be: 'weight to the left, ball to the right'.

In a stressful situation, the simpler and more concise the mnemonic, the more chance there is of remembering it.

• Using onomatopoeia

We have seen how the knowledge of techniques tends to be centred in the left hemisphere of your brain, whilst the right hemisphere reacts more to stimuli such as rhythms, sensations and images. If you say to someone, 'Hit the ball', sharply and with every word clearly enunciated, the message is much more likely to get through than if you tell them in great detail how to accelerate the head of their club. Timothy Gallwey introduced the famous, and highly onomatopoeic phrase, 'back-hit'. Many other words have been used to help pupils with the three different speeds involved in the swing. Some people recommend quietly saying 'oom..pa..pah' to yourself as you play the shot. Another commonly used phrase is 'ladies and gentlemen', which beautifully encapsulates the rhythm of the swing.

Other words are used in specific situations: for example, Gary Wiren advises thinking or saying the word 'splash' when playing out of a bunker, and thinking about the word 'leaf' when putting, to keep your grip as light as possible. When Sam Snead swings, he thinks about the word 'oil', and Bob Toski imagines a canoe sliding down from the crest to the trough of a wave.

● Imitation

It is a well-known fact that children have extraordinary powers of imitation, which they gradually lose as they grow older. Only a selected few maintain this ability into adulthood. Sometimes it is useful if you imitate the mistake the pupil is making so that they can see it more clearly. Alternatively, if you show them a picture of the shot in a book they may find it easier to relate to.

Some pros tell their pupils to hold the club with their left hand and then put their own right hand on the grip. This means that the pupil can see how the movement should be carried out. This is an interesting method, because it involves several basic principles of educational theory: imitation, awareness of mistakes and new sensations.

● Exaggerating mistakes

Another modern psychological theory, called systemic therapy, involves forcing the person to repeat and exaggerate their mistake until they become aware of it. In sex therapy, if a man is anxious and has a fear of impotence, he is told to deliberately try to be impotent. Sometimes this method, originally developed by the German psychoanalyst Wilhelm Stekel in the 1930s, is miraculously successful because the man no longer feels he *has* to succeed.

The same idea could be used in golf with pupils who are tense, overuse their right hands and therefore constantly mis-hit shots. Try telling them to deliberately play a hook or a slice. This makes the pupil consciously aware of their mistake, and by activating their opposite side, the mistake will often disappear as if by magic.

● Teaching by metaphor

Children are naturally at home with metaphors, and are often talked to using images. When dealing with adults, we often tend to explain concepts in concrete, practical terms which are analysed by the left-hand side of the brain. But as we know, both sides of the brain need to be used in parallel if teaching is to be effective, and in cases like these, a metaphor can be very useful.

To use a personal example, my friend Gerry had reached senior age and was afraid of not being able to hit the ball as far as he had used to. This meant he had a habit of over-swinging to lengthen his drive. I watched him taking lessons from a pro, Bill Reid, who taught him a wholly new concept: the speed of the club depends on the resistance it meets as you swing it. If he moved his feet or head, there would not be enough resistance and the ball would not travel fast enough. My friend was still unable to understand how he could speed up the head of his club by increasing the amount of resistance to the movement, since this seemed to be a contradiction in terms. So I suggested the metaphor of the water in a river. When a river is flowing between two banks which are fairly wide apart, the current will be fairly slow. But if the banks become narrower, the water will flow faster. If you imagine your feet and head as the two banks and your club as the water, it is that much easier to understand that if you increase the amount of resistance, you will also increase the speed of the club.

Teaching by metaphor is an essential skill in modern-day psychology, and all too often its importance in golf coaching is underestimated.

● Listening

There are many other psychological principles which will help you teach golf effectively. Like a psychoanalyst or a priest, you need to be very patient and have very good listening skills. It is often boring to hear the same comments being made by one pupil after another thinking they are the first person ever to say them.

Likewise, if you as the coach spend too much of your time talking and showing off your own ability, you are ignoring one of the fundamental principles of any form of teaching: the most important thing is to listen.

Another friend of mine who was an antiques dealer was often visited by well-off women with nothing to do all day but sit and tell him their woes. However, his reward for being such a good listener was that being listened to made them more likely to spend their money in his shop.

● Conclusion: the pro as facilitator

In clinical psychology there are many different methods available to the therapist, ranging from the active didacticism of behavioural therapy to the benevolent neutrality of Freudian psychoanalysis. Between these two extremes is the idea of the therapist as *facilitator*, which is advocated by gestalt therapy. I think this is the method which is most appropriate to golf teaching. A pro should help pupils plan for their training and go through the exercises with them. Always try to anticipate pupils' problems, and be flexible so that you can react to events as they happen. If a pupil is under stress you should recognize this by stopping them and suggesting ways of becoming aware of this tension and dealing with it.

Rigorous but not rigid; authoritative but not authoritarian; flexible but not lax. These qualities are the hallmarks of a golf coach who acts as a facilitator and sets pupils realistic objectives which are neither too hard nor too easy. Essentially, you should be in tune with your pupil's unconscious.

How to Learn

The previous chapter described some of the psychological factors that should play a part in good golf teaching. This chapter turns the tables and looks at learning golf from the pupil's angle.

● Deliberate mistakes

One way of understanding why you are making a mistake is to deliberately try to make it again. This somewhat paradoxical idea is often used in psychology. In Jacobson's relaxation technique, instead of being told to relax, patients are asked to tense their muscles as much as possible until they are exhausted by the tension, and then feel what it is like to relax. We have already described this idea in the previous chapter, but you may also want to learn it on your own, in between teaching sessions.

If you are making a mistake (such as slicing) and do not know why, try to do it again deliberately. This will help to make you aware of the movements you are carrying out when you make the mistake. Often, slices are the result of your forearm being too tense and your right hand holding the grip too hard.

So try to play the slice again and work out exactly where it is going wrong.

Psychologically, if you deliberately do something wrong you are sending a false message to the left-hand side of your brain and freeing up the right hemisphere. If you are successful with this exercise, you will join the hallowed ranks of those who only play slices or hooks when they want to.

● Anticipating the result

Learning may not be effective if you try to squeeze it into too little time or make it last too long. All of us are impatient and like to see rapid results. Even if your teacher is doing a perfectly good job, their hard work may be going to waste if you fail to accept that learning takes time. Often you will make no progress at all for weeks, and then suddenly start improving. This is particularly true of children, who learn not in linear fashion but in stages.

If you can avoid hurrying your learning, this will help you avoid the common mistake of ignoring good shots and therefore gradually forgetting them. Another potential pitfall is working so hard on correcting your mistakes that you neglect your good points, with the net result that your scores remain unchanged.

• Using onomatopoeia

In the previous chapter on teaching golf, we described different ways of using the sound and rhythm of words to control the rhythm of your play. Read this section if you have not done so already, and then try the method yourself.

• Bit by bit or all in one go?

Both of these methods have their uses, and how you learn will depend a great deal on your own particular abilities. It can often be useful to break down a particular shot into sections and then analyse these one at a time. One way of improving your golf is to work on the left-hand side of your brain: how your arm should move in relation to the lower half of your body, and vice versa, how to swing into rather than hit the ball, and how to finish a shot. Breaking a technique down into its component parts brings the left hemisphere of your brain into play, even if it is only to set a sequence of finite objectives.

But other learners will find the opposite process more beneficial: to view a movement as a single whole. If you are able to imagine the whole of your swing as a unit, you may well find it easier to resolve problems with it. This is an application of the gestalt principle to golf: seeing concepts as a whole rather than as the sum of their parts.

One way of viewing a shot as a whole is to picture someone else you know, perhaps from your club or on TV, who is good at playing that particular shot. One friend of mine says the easiest way to get out of a bunker is to say to himself: 'Swing like Sam Snead does'. Or if you have problems with your short game, you might do well to imagine Seve Ballesteros in a similar situation. A single mental image is often much more effective than trying to remember a long list of highly technical instructions.

• Keeping a psychological scorecard

One excellent way of monitoring the psychological factors which affect the way you play is to take notes as you go round the course. On a card, write down the direction and length of each shot, the number of shots which ended up in bunkers, in the water or out-of-bounds, and also the number of putts you take. Then jot down the way you feel about each hole after playing it, focusing on your state of mind and any muscular tension that may have occurred.

● Visual and sensory learning

Another way of training your mind is to analyse how you perceive things in everyday life: whether you perceive things in sensory terms, or in terms of visual images.

Every one of us has a different way of perceiving reality, based on our own personal experience. For example, imagine you are hungry and about to tuck into a meal. Do you notice the smell of the food and the way it tastes on your tongue, or do you picture the shape and colour of the food itself? With the exception of a very few people who see reality in both sensory and visual terms, most of us divide fairly neatly into one camp or the other. As a golf player, there is no point learning techniques visually if you are basically a sensory person, or vice versa.

Perhaps an example from my own clinical experience will explain this concept better. A couple came to see me for marriage guidance counselling, their main problems apparently being sexual ones. The husband accused the wife of shying away from sex. He said she was frigid because, in his words, 'I've brought her home some adult videos and they don't have any effect on her at all!' His wife countered that she preferred being touched, because she was more sensitive to physical sensations than to visual images. This was much more of a communication prob-lem than a sexual one. In the same way, it is important not to learn golf using methods which you do not appreciate because they use the wrong frame of reference.

The following test shows how this principle works in practice by making you imagine various types of shot (drive, chip, pitch, sand wedge and putt). In each case, there are different ways of imagining the situation: either in terms of technique, or in sensory or visual terms.

Example 1

Imagine you have hit a lightly sliced drive into the rough to the right of a par-4 hole which dog-legs to the right. You now have to play a 9 iron over a clump of trees to try and reach the green. Concentrate on the shot (but don't go through the motions), close your eyes and answer the following five questions:

a. How far above the trees did your ball go?
b. Did it fall long or short of the green?
c. How many times did it bounce?
d. Was there a wind blowing, and if so from which direction?
e. What type of tree was it that the ball went over?

Now answer the following questions:

a. Did you feel tense or anxious?
b. If so, which part of your body felt most tense?
c. Could you give it a score on a scale from 1 to 10?

d. Was the 9 iron heavy or light? Were you gripping it tightly?

Now look at your replies to see whether you feel more at ease with the first set of questions (visual) or the second (sensory and physical). If necessary, give each point a percentage depending on how important it is. Then test yourself with the following example.

Example 2
You are on the green at your local club and about to play a downhill putt of about 10 feet which will break from right to left. Look at the green, line up the shot and answer the following questions:

a. Did the ball roll evenly?
b. Was the green dry or damp?
c. What colour was the flag?

Now answer the following questions:

a. How tightly did you grip the club?
b. Did you hit the ball or stroke it?
c. Do you feel it went past the hole or went in?

Use these answers to decide which type of perception comes easier to you: whether you are more sensory, or more visual.

Once you have done this, ask yourself some further questions:

a. When I'm playing well, do I make more use of feelings or images?
b. When I'm playing badly, am I more likely to lose control of feelings, images or both?
c. When I'm playing badly, do I tend to use feelings or images to get myself back on an even keel? Or neither?
d. If I want to make progress, do I need to improve my weak side (sensory or visual) or do I need to strengthen my strong side?

If you are still not quite sure, read the following sections on technique and the mind.

The Swing

• Using your mind when you swing

In this and the following two sections, we will apply some of the psychological techniques you have learned to the actual movements of golf. As you go through the different stages of the swing (the address, the grip, the waggle, the forward press, the backswing, downswing, strike and follow-through), you can either set yourself specific objectives in terms of the techniques you use, or you can set yourself objectives using psycho-golf.

We have already described the psy-

chological importance of the rituals many golfers use. Always using particular clubs, a particular colour of tee or a particular numbered ball are all ways of relieving the tensions and stresses that occur in golf.

Other players attain a state of active relaxation by controlling their breathing, checking their physical sensations (such as muscle tension and skin temperature), or by using mental images.

Before we analyse the various psychological aspects of the swing, there are three important principles which can help you reduce your levels of anxiety and tension.

a. If you focus on swinging your club rather than on hitting the ball, this will give you a greater likelihood of success.

In the chapter on teaching golf, we showed how the more tense and anxious you are about wanting to hit the ball as hard as you can, the less far the ball is likely to go. It is quite possible to hit the ball with only 80 per cent of your potential strength and for it to travel just as far as one hit with 100 per cent of your strength, simply because your swing is more relaxed the first time and makes up for the lack of strength. One analogy is with the fable of the oak tree and the reed. When a gale blows, the oak has much greater resistance, but at the height of the gale the oak is uprooted, whereas the reed bends in the wind and rights itself again afterwards. The moral of this story is that your strength is measured just as much in how flexible you are as in how rigid you are.

b. Your confidence at the start of a game can affect the whole of the rest of the game. Jack Nicklaus points out in his book, *Golf my Way*, that when you tee off at the first hole, it is vital not to hesitate over which club to use, and choose the one you feel most confident with, rather than the one which you feel will hit the ball furthest. A game of golf lasts perhaps three to four hours, and it would be a shame to ruin it from the word go just because you are too obstinate to select a club you feel comfortable with.

c. Being familiar with the technique of the swing is not a sure-fire guarantee of success, especially if you use the wrong rhythm and tempo and the different stages are not linked together in a smooth movement. When you are on the course, forget the objectives you set yourself when you were practising and instead concentrate on the physical symptoms referred to above: breathing, muscle tension, sweaty palms, and so on.

● General images

The swing is not a movement that comes naturally to most people, but there are a number of ways which will help you to picture it in your mind. The following exercises and ideas from championship players may be of some help.

• Give colours to the different stages of the swing and the different parts of your body. Imagine the active parts of your body being red, and the relaxed parts blue. Imagine the inside of your legs as being red to remind you to keep the weight of your body focused on this area. Imagine these two colours being reversed as you first swing the club backwards and then forwards, and this will help you transfer your bodyweight.

Another possibility is to give different colours to different parts of the swing. For example, you could imagine the putter accelerating into a red area surrounding the ball.

• One traditional way of making sure you transfer your weight properly is to use the image of your legs forming a

Your right leg should be doing all the work in the backswing, and your left in the downswing. This means shifting the weight of your body.

Right **Place your legs in a double K to make it easier to pivot.**

Below **Proper balance from the beginning to the end of the swing is essential, even if you are playing from an unusual situation.**

double K. During the backswing, your left knee should move to the right; in the downswing, the opposite movement should take place.

• A good swing must have balance and rhythm. A good way of remembering this is to imagine that you are balanced on a log raft and your club is the rope of a child's swing.

• If you are to swing properly, it is also important not to sway during the backswing or move the top half of your body in the downswing. One good idea is to imagine yourself swinging the club with your body between two stakes in the ground.

If you have mastered the basics of swinging, you may also want to imagine

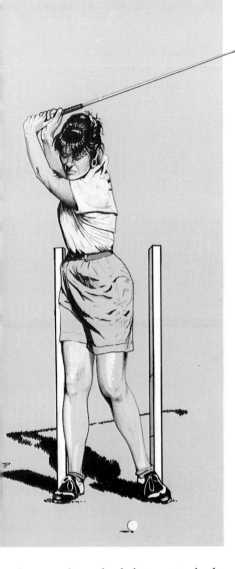

To avoid swaying from side to side and to keep your body weight centred between your legs, imagine swinging between two fixed posts.

Try to hit the dark-coloured part of the ball to help you use an in-out movementin the downswing.

the top of your body being attached to a pole which stops you from moving but allows your thighs and legs to move freely.

• Nearly all good golfers, whatever stance they adopt in the set-up, tend to hit the ball along an in-out axis. Again, this is not a movement that comes easily, and there are two images you might use to visualize it:

a. Imagine the ball divided into four with the lower right-hand side painted a different colour to remind you which part of the ball to hit.

b. Alternatively, imagine yourself swinging the club across the face of a clock. Despite what you might think, a good swing should be played along a line not from 6 to 12 o'clock, but from 7 to 1 o'clock.

c. A good solid swing should be centred on your left-hand side during the backswing and downswing, and your right hand should only take on the dominant role after you have hit the ball. This principle is often hard for beginners and people who find it difficult to use their left arm to control the club. One way of improving this situation is to play the same swing with a specific grip but not close your right

Exactly the same thing applies to the swing: if you suddenly lose your visual feedback, you will be more aware of the importance of swinging into the ball rather than just hitting it.

• Some teachers, known as the 'mentalists', tell pupils to make a swing and rate the amount of tension they feel on a scale of one to ten. This consciousness-raising exercise can be used for other shots in golf as well.

• Before you start a game, or if you are going through a stressful time, you might try running through a checklist of the tension in your hands, your forearms and your neck, and make sure your neck is straight. Check that your feet are firmly planted on the ground and make sure you shift your weight onto your right leg in the backswing and onto your left leg in the downswing. Another thing you could try is to imagine that the club is extremely light and weighs only a few grammes at the moment you begin your swing.

• One way of gaining a better perception of the shift in your weight from one leg to the other is to be aware of the sensations your brain receives from the soles of your feet, in the same way as skiers do. Instead of waggling your hands, do the same with your feet by using little movements shifting your weight back and forth between your feet. This exercise is often useful if you shift your weight the wrong way as you swing, in other words from your left to your right leg. This often results in a slice or a lob.

To strengthen the left side, press your right hand onto the grip, keeping the hand open.

hand on the club again. This will bring home how important your left-hand side is when you swing.

• General sensations

• Timothy Gallwey suggests playing a swing (not just the short game and the putt) with your eyes shut. In everyday life, visual feedback often dominates our perceptions to the point where we ignore other sense impressions. You can demonstrate this to yourself next time you are out on the course by standing amongst some trees for a few minutes and shutting your eyes. After a few moments you will start to be aware of smells you had not noticed before, hear the sounds of woodland life and feeling the ground beneath your feet.

• If you are tense, there is a tendency to lose your awareness of the blade of your club and how fast it is travelling. This awareness is one of the features which often distinguishes the good players from the not-so-good. If you want to regain your awareness of your swing, try taking your driver and hitting the ball only half the normal distance but using the full movement of the swing. Now try gradually hitting the ball further and further by speeding up the movement. This is also a very good exercise for regaining your tempo.

• The noise of the shaft moving through the air can also provide useful sensory feedback. Golf Digest suggests holding your club by the blade, or even using a fishing-rod, and going through the normal movements of a swing. The noise the club makes as it whips through the air should come from your right-hand side, because the club should be at maximum acceleration as the club moves downwards, not after you have hit the ball.

If you hold your club upside-down and whip it through the air, it will help you feel the sensation of accelerating the club prior to impact with the ball.

The interlocking grip for short fingers or weaker hands

The little finger of the right hand and the index finger of the left hand are crossed. Jack Nicklaus uses this grip.

The overlapping grip - the most common form

The little finger of the right hand is placed between the index finger and the long finger of the left hand.

The baseball grip - now rarely used

All ten fingers are separated and each one touches the club.
This grip is not recommended as it gives poor club control.

• The grip

A reminder of the technique

A good grip is the most important part of golfing technique: you need only watch a professional carefully position-ing their hands on the shaft, and then watch an amateur doing the same thing without giving it a moment's thought. You will also find it is harder to change a bad grip than other aspects of your technique.

Gripping the club

Put your left hand in place first: this is the key to a good grip. The handle of the club should rest diagonally across the palm of your left hand and in the fingers of your right hand. The index finger of your right hand should form a kind of trigger on the handle by placing your thumb on the top of the grip without extending it. One way of checking that your grip is right is to make sure that the V formed by the thumb and index finger of each hand points towards your right shoulder.

The main pressure should be exerted by the last three fingers of your left hand. A good grip should be light, but also firm.

Images to help you improve your grip

The following three images are often used:

BAD GRIPS

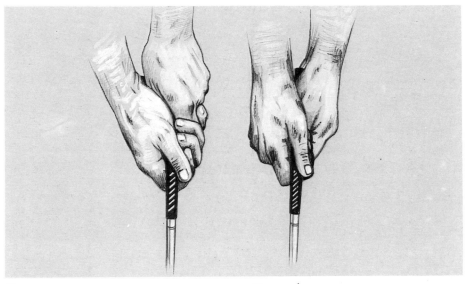

Too strong
Gripping the club too hard causes a hook because the hands are too far round to the right. The right hand is near the bottom of the grip and closes the clubface on impact.

Too weak
The hands are too far round to the left, with the thumb and index finger of each hand forming a V pointing towards the left shoulder. This gives a weak grip which opens the clubface on impact and causes a slice.

• Instead of gripping the club, imagine you are gripping a small bird between your hands.
• Alternatively, imagine a more familiar object, such as a tube of toothpaste.
• One good way of helping you to relax is to imagine that your hands are resting on a cushion.

There is an anecdote about Bob Toski shaking a pupil's hand as he began his first lesson at a very expensive golf clinic. 'Hi, I'm Bob Toski', he said. 'That handshake just cost you $100!' As the pupil's jaw dropped, Toski

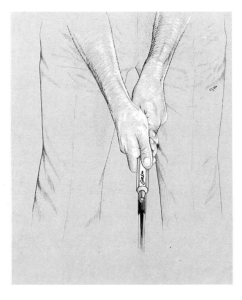

Never grip the club more tightly than you would a tube of toothpaste!

• Address Stance Alignment

Many shots can be affected by poor address. Imagine a set square placed between your feet to help you line up properly.

added: 'Never grip your club any harder than I just gripped your hand'.

A reminder of the technique
Posture
Stand as though you are about to sit down; only your legs should be bent. Distribute your body weight evenly across your two feet; relax your neck, keep your back flat and point your buttocks slightly away from the target.

Place the ball either centred in your stance or in line with the heel of your left foot, depending on the club you are using. Your position should be confident, but not too relaxed. Ideally, your hips should tilt slightly to the right and your arms should be flexible, but not taut.

Stance
Your stance is the way your feet are positioned and spaced in relation to the ball's direction of travel. When playing long shots, your feet should be at least a shoulders' width apart; bring them closer together for short shots. There are three possible positions:

The square stance
Keep your two feet parallel to an imaginary line joining the tips of both feet to the hole.

The closed stance
Keep your right foot back from your left when playing long shots (woods and long irons) to make it easier to swivel as you backswing or play a hook.

The open stance

Keep your left foot back from your right for short (7, 8 or 9) irons in the short game, in bunkers (using a 10 or sand wedge), or to play a slice.

Your **alignment** should be controlled by your shoulders and hips, which should be parallel to the ball's line of travel. If need be, check that your feet are properly aligned by placing a club on the ground pointing towards the hole and line up your feet with it.

Visualizing the set-up

To improve your set-up, imagine a set square with one edge along your feet, and your club should be in line with the perpendicular edge. You could practise this by identifying a target on the course. Alternatively, choose a point a few metres away along the axis of the target and the line of the ball. If you suffer from the common tendency to line up too far to the right this precaution will help you.

Many golfers are too hunched when they line up; the ideal position is one of controlled relaxation. If your stance is weak, try imagining you are a boxer or a tennis player.

If in doubt, keep your stance square. This will help you line up.

Stand in a posture of active relaxation in the address, like a boxer or a tennis player.

There are also various animals with highly symbolic connotations which may help you as an anxious golfer. If you are tense you will tend to hunch your shoulders, making it difficult for them to turn. Try imagining you are a giraffe eating leaves from a tall tree.

If you have problems with muscle tension throughout the lower half of your body and are therefore not properly anchored to the ground, imagine that your legs are very heavy, like those of an elephant.

If you are tense as you line up for a shot, you will not be able to use your feet to test that your weight is properly distributed across your legs. If this happens, waggling your feet instead of your hands may be helpful. If you find you are not transferring your weight across onto your right foot because you are afraid of swaying, try lining up with your right shoe off so that you can distinguish the different feelings through your feet.

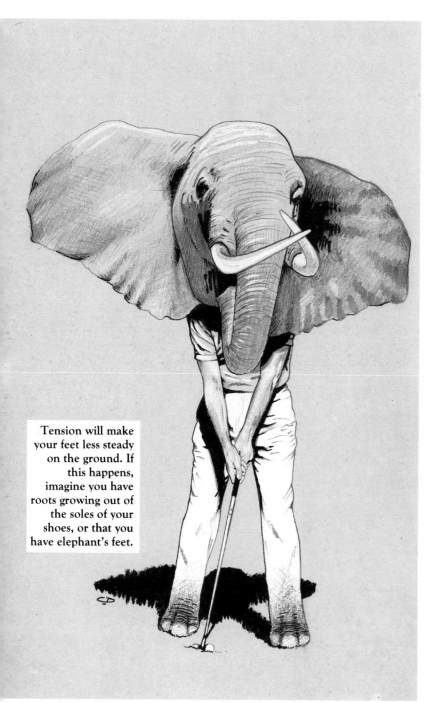

Tension will make your feet less steady on the ground. If this happens, imagine you have roots growing out of the soles of your shoes, or that you have elephant's feet.

● The backswing

A reminder of the technique

Start with a waggle to relax your wrists and then a forward press to start the swing. Different people do this in different ways. The backswing should be controlled by your left shoulder, with your left arm acting as an extension to the shaft and making the blade of the club run parallel with the ground for about 8 inches. Then start swinging your body as well until the club has come up to the horizontal; keep your left arm taut and your wrists flexible. At the end of the backswing, you should be in the following position:

- Shoulders swung through 90°;
- Hips pivoted 45°;
- Body weight divided as follows:
    70 per cent inside your right heel
    30 per cent inside the tip of your left foot;
- Left heel slightly off the ground;
- Knees relaxed;
- Eyes constantly on the ball (this is very important);
- Left shoulder to the right of the ball.

If you are short, it is best to use a flat plane for the backswing (like Gary Player or Lee Trevino, for example) to give you more leverage and therefore hit the ball harder. But if you are a taller player, like Johnny Miller, use a more upright backswing to give you more control.

Exactly how you play the backswing will depend on the club you use: the

short game will need a more upright backswing, whilst longer clubs will require more of an inclined plane.

The image of turning within a cylinder will improve your backswing.

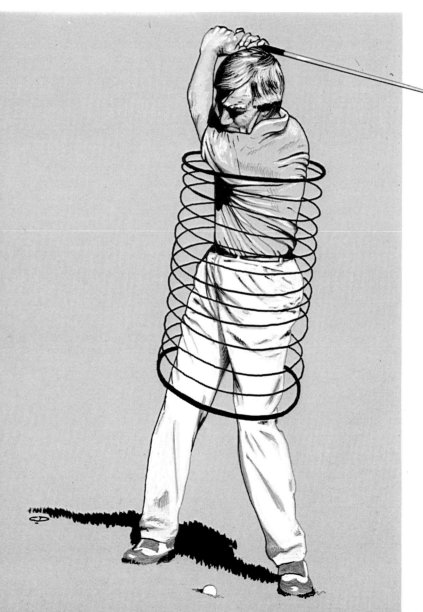

Images to help your backswing

• Learning to turn your body rather than your hands and arms is essential for a good swing, because it allows you to build up energy; one image that may remind you of this is that of a coiled spring. Most pros start their backswing with their left shoulder. Tom Watson recommends starting the backswing compact, left shoulders and left hip together. It is important that you visualize these parts of your body and identify the messages they are sending you.

One image that may help to remind you of the proper way to swivel your body to the right is to imagine playing inside a barrel without touching the sides.

• At the end of this movement, it may help you to imagine your hands high up in the clouds; this is much easier to visualize than being told to swivel through 90° because the latter immediately brings the analytical left-hand side of your brain into play.

• At the top of the backswing and to help you start your downswing properly, try imagining yourself changing gear when you reach the top of a hill. Alternatively, imagine you are a waiter carrying a tray of drinks on your club and starting your downswing without spilling the drunks. This will stop you from starting the downswing with your right shoulder.

Left **Imagine your hands in the clouds at the top of the backswing.**

Below **Make sure you co-ordinate the shift in bodyweight with your hand movements.**

10 kg

100 kg

500 kg

• The downswing

A reminder of the technique

Use the lower half of your body (feet, legs, thighs, hips) for the downswing. Move your hips sideways to the left, shift your body weight onto your left leg, bring your arms down keeping your wrists taut, and do all this without moving your head. As you move close to hitting the ball, uncoil your hips and relax your wrists so that your hands can start to rotate: this is important to give you distance.

- Shift your body weight to the left,
- Lift the heel of your right foot and pivot on the point of your foot,
- Turn your hips towards the target,
- Keep both arms fully stretched immediately after hitting the ball,
- Keep your head still all the time.

Useful images

- Imagine starting the downswing

with your hands as though you were pulling on a bell rope. This will prevent you from starting too high with your right shoulder and therefore causing an out-in movement. Alternatively, place a tee in the top of the grip and imagine you are going to bury it in the ground. The other alternative is not to follow this advice at all, but to start the downswing with the lower half of your body.

• To help you begin your downswing by shifting your weight to the left, imagine someone pulling on the left-hand pocket of your trousers. Better still, picture yourself moving along a set of rails so that you can only move sideways in one direction.

• To make the club work for you during the downswing and increase its speed, imagine that the club is very

Picture a tee in the end of your club shaft and bring it down towards the ball. You should still twist the lower half of your body in the downswing.

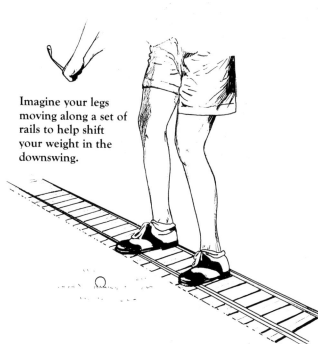

Imagine your legs moving along a set of rails to help shift your weight in the downswing.

heavy and that the ball is a beach ball; hit it so that it rotates inwards.

• To keep the movement consistent and fast until you hit the ball, try using the image of a boxer hitting a punchbag or a lumberjack burying his axe in a tree.

There are two other images which may help you to achieve the same objective. Imagine yourself slamming a door at the moment that you hit the ball, or pretend you are practising karate by

smashing a wooden plank instead of the ball.

Another way of giving the head of the club the maximum acceleration is to imagine that the ball is on the finishing line of a dog track and has to keep pace with the dogs crossing the line at high speed.

One other possibility is to use the same image as before, of the barrel, but this time imagine smashing the barrel with your downswing.

• The speed of the club will depend on a variety of factors, but one thing which will certainly increase it is keeping your head still. One way of staying behind the ball is to keep your eyes fixed on the tee even after the club has hit the ball.

Visualize the ball turning into a beach ball and make it spin to the left; this will give you a better finish.

A strong, accurate shot needs to be hit firmly, with the club accelerating through the ball. These are some of the images you might use: the finishing line at a dog track, a punch in karate, chopping a log or smashing your way out of a barrel.

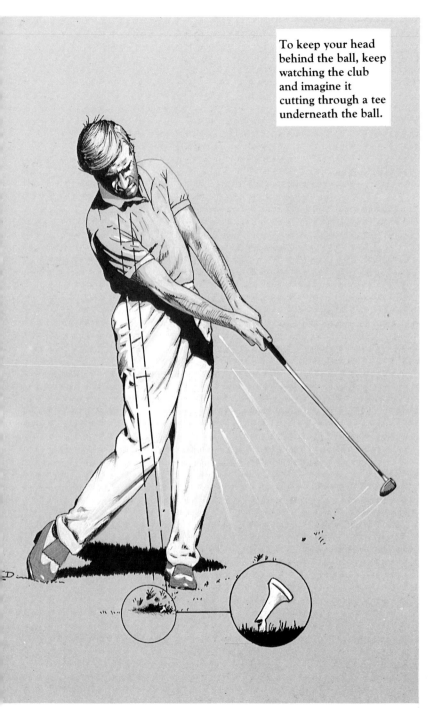

To keep your head behind the ball, keep watching the club and imagine it cutting through a tee underneath the ball.

● The finish

A reminder of the technique

The finish is an essential part of a good swing which is a solid, well-constructed movement. If you lose your balance at the end of a swing, it is because your backswing was wrong and your downswing started too high. This will cause a slice or a hook, or possibly a straight but short shot. So at the end of the swing, you should be in the following position:

- Facing towards the target;
- Left leg straight and right leg bent;
- Hands high;
- The whole of your body weight on your left leg;
- Left foot pointing outwards;
- Right heel completely off the ground with your foot swivelled on your toes.

Images to help you with your finish

Not all champion golfers have the same finish. Some prefer to finish with their hands well up; others have their hands turned more towards the left. If you prefer to keep your hands high, try using the image of the double umbrella. If you have your hands high at the end of the backswing, you should have them just as high at the end of the swing, in a mirror-image reversal.

Other teachers advise their pupils to pretend they are throwing a bucket of water. This movement should end with your hands high and parallel.

To make your finish a natural extension of a smooth downswing as far as your hands are concerned, you might want to use the idea of hitch-hiking, with your left hand. You start with your thumb extended to the right as the car approaches, and then swivel your thumb as the car gets closer to indicate that you want to go towards your left.

Another way of remembering the proper hand movement is to picture the buckle on your belt turning round sideways until it faces the target as you finish the shot.

Whichever method you use, if your swing is to be consistent your hands must be firm, as though they are chained together until the end of the movement. Your posture at the end of the finish should be confident: don't huddle up in a ball. One way of reminding yourself to keep your head up is to imagine that you are taking a photo of the ball.

Left **If you complete the swing properly with your hands parallel and high up, you will not spill any of the water to either side.**

Below **Another way of obtaining a good finish is to picture the buckle of your belt facing the target. Finish with your head held high as though posing for a photograph.**

Finally, there is one important thing to point out at the end of this chapter on the swing. I have given you dozens of ideas and exercises to use, but don't try working your way through the whole list while you are on the course. Just choose one or two which suit your own particular situation.

The Short Game

● Learning to live with stress

Whether you are trying for a birdie or struggling to save par, the short game has its own particular technical and psychological difficulties. Whole books have been written on the subject, and its importance is shown by the fact that as they grow older, experienced golfers can still maintain their handicap by improving the quality of their short game. The big difference between a pro and a good amateur is their shots on and around the green, despite the fact that many people still regard the length of a player's drive as one of the main indicators of how good they are.

In this part of the game, good technique is of prime importance. Different teachers will tell you different things: play with or without your wrist, change clubs for rolled approaches or use the same club but with a shorter backswing, and so on. Despite these differences of opinion, it is universally agreed that in the short game dexterity is more important than strength and in theory, young players, women and seniors all have an equal chance.

When results do vary, it is more likely to be because of a whole number of minor factors which are difficult to quantify. Good use of muscular dexterity, listening to what your feelings tell you and confidence will all help you to improve your game.

If you are to succeed in your short game, it is vital to listen and understand before you act. All too often, golfers want to be told what to do rather than playing by instinct.

Some of the problems particular to the short game are these:

● Arriving near the green rattled by mistakes you have just made.
● Swinging stiffly because you have dropped a shot and want to get it back or striving for a birdie by way of a good approach and single putt.
● Being dangerously close to the area where you are 'expected to succeed'.
● Having a clearer idea of exactly where it is you are aiming for, which gives you less room to manoeuvre than in other shots.
● Being less aware of muscle tension than in the long game; this reduced feedback gives you less of a chance to correct problems.

- Finally, the course itself can raise your stress levels, because the main obstacles tend to be located round the green in the short game area. Many modern courses are well known not only for their length, but also because there are so many hazards around the green.

• Bunkers

General problems

Golf was first developed in Scotland, and was often played by the sea, which is why sand plays such an important part in the golf course. As time went on, it was recognized as being an essential feature of any course, with the emphasis on the area around the green but also on the fairway.

Sand can very easily become an obsessive fear for many golfers; the more you try to avoid it, the more you seem to end up in it. But most professionals will tell you that getting out of a bunker is much easier than you might think, and you can actually turn sand to your advantage by using it to create backspin. Despite this, for many golfers sand is something which they are afraid of, and it is easy to lose your competitive advantage in a bunker. Another problem is that it is hard to tell which of your problems are real and which are subjective.

- There are a number of unknown quantities in a bunker, including the quality, thickness and consistency of the sand. Some bunkers use such fine sand that you sink into it, which decreases the distance between your hands and the ball. Conversely, if it has recently rained or the course has been watered, you may need to adapt your technique accordingly.
- When you are playing in a bunker, it is impossible to go through the normal pre-swing rituals. You cannot play a practice swing because you cannot ground your club. This increases your anxiety and muscular tension as you are unable to perform the rituals you normally take for granted, and you also lose the reassurance of the forward press.
- The textbooks will tell you that you should aim to hit not the ball, but the sand behind it, so that the sand itself blasts the ball onto the green. But as a beginner, the natural thing to do is the opposite and you end up by scooping the ball out. It often takes a great deal of thought to exchange normal logic for golfing logic.

- Most golfers stuck in a bunker set themselves over-ambitious objectives given the amount of risk involved and their own abilities. Forget the idea of dropping the ball neatly by the pin from the bunker; leave this to the professionals. If you concentrate on getting the ball onto the green, your shot will almost certainly be more relaxed and more effective.

A reminder of the technique

Like other forms of play, bunker shots have their own special techniques. These vary from one teacher to another and one situation to another, but the underlying principles are these:

- Normally you should use the sand wedge, because it is more open and heavy: open because it needs to bring the ball upwards more than forwards, and heavy because it needs to go into the sand;
- Stand in an open stance;
- Shift the weight of your body slightly to the left;
- Keep your hands slightly forward of the head of the club;
- Make sure your feet are firmly anchored on the ground;
- Break your wrists as you backswing;
- Don't swivel your shoulders as much as you would normally, and bring the club more upright than usual;
- Try to move through the shot and end up with your weight on your left foot.

In a bunker on the fairway, you can use a more powerful club (a 5–6 iron or a 5 wood). The main thing is to gain as much distance as possible. Hit the ball cleanly and take account of the height of the face of the bunker in front of you and the lie of the ball.

Special bunker shots

If your ball is plugged in the sand, do the following:

• Always take up the same position;

• Hold the face of the club more closed than usual;

• Break your wrists at the beginning of the backswing;

• In the downswing, you need to approach the ball at a fairly acute angle to get the head of the club underneath the ball. Even if the head of your club closes as it hits the ball (this is quite normal), make sure you transfer your body weight well onto your left leg.

If the lip of the bunker is just behind your ball, use the same technique as you would for a plugged ball, unless you need to open the face of the club as much as possible.

If the ball is just in front of the rim of the bunker, 'blast' it by blocking the shot on impact and not following through.

Whichever position the ball is in, you will only become a good bunker player if you use both your feet and your hands; both are vital for a successful shot.

Exercises for sensory learners

If you tend to think of things in terms of their effect on your senses rather than on your vision, try some of the following ideas for dealing with bunkers.

• Before you go into the bunker yourself, breathe deeply at least three times, with the emphasis on breathing out

using your abdominal muscles. If you are anxious, this will make you hunch your shoulders and breathe in more deeply, which in turn will encourage your muscles to contract rather than relax. Breathing out hard and long, using your abdomen, will bring your shoulders down and make them independent of your head and therefore more able to turn freely. It will also help you to relax your muscles.

• Once you are in the bunker, it is important to check the tension of your forearms and hands; eight times out of ten, you will be holding the club too tightly. Try rating the firmness of your grip on a scale of one to five so that you become aware of it before you hit the shot, not after you have played it. If you are still tense, try some of the basic relaxation techniques described earlier in the book. For example, you might try a technique from Jacobson's relaxation by holding the club as tightly as

you possibly can and then letting go. This means you can compare the two extremes: first gripping the club as hard as possible, and then as loosely as you can, in order to find the half-way point. Too tight a grip will restrict the freedom of your wrists and your ability to get through the sand and underneath the ball, whilst too soft a grip will not resist the impact with the ground.

• There is also a bunker exercise which will help reduce problems with moving sand. Try shuffling back and forth to explore the texture of the sand as though you were walking barefoot. You will gradually feel you are on more familiar, welcoming territory. You might also try wielding the club without the ball, just to get a feel for playing out of a bunker. Experiment with the club for a couple of minutes in the bunker and imagine different ways of getting the ball out. Estimate the weight of the sand that will be displaced, the amount of resistance it will provide to the club and the direction it will go when you hit it. This will help you to feel more at home in the bunker and give you more confidence.

One good practice technique is to try playing the shot with your eyes closed, focusing on the feeling you get and then trying to work out where the ball has landed. Then open your eyes and see how much difference there is between expectations and reality.

If the worst comes to the worst, say or think the word 'splash' as you swing and hope the right hemisphere of your brain is listening.

Exercises for visual people

The following exercises can be adapted to your specific situation once you have identified the problems you want to solve.

• If you cannot visualize the whole of your body and your swing when playing in a bunker, try imagining your favourite player playing the shot for you.

• If you are obsessed with hitting the ball and afraid of hitting the sand, you may like to imagine that you are trying to scoop up a fried egg or a cake from the bunker and drop it gently on the green.

• If you are over-anxious, and tension in your forearms makes you hurry your downswing, imagine the ball replaced by a glass of wine on a tray and try to place it on the green without spilling a drop.

Two suggestions made by Golf Digest are that you imagine a little child sitting on the face of your club, or a bucket of water which you have to balance without tipping it over. The aim of all these images is to short-circuit your active wish to hit the ball and instead use exercises which help you to develop a light, rhythmical movement by analogy.

• Finally, another way of helping you to overcome your fear of getting underneath the ball is to imagine that the ball is placed on a tee buried in the sand. The object of the exercise is to try and cut the tee in two with the blade of your club. In training, you

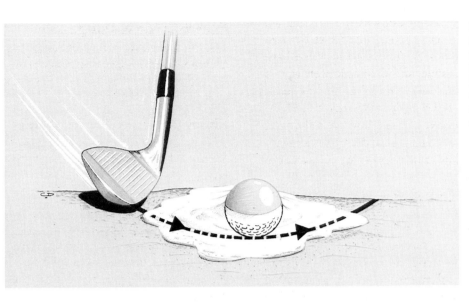

Left One way of getting the club into the sand is to imagine that the ball is an egg yolk which you are trying to drop on the green without breaking it.

Below If you are trying to play a delicate bunker shot and avoid closing the clubface, imagine the ball is a glass of wine and you are placing it on the green.

could even do this exercise by placing an actual tee underneath the ball.

● Chipping

Most of the points mentioned in the general introduction apply to the stressful situation of chipping. You have to rectify a fault you have already made, you have a precise objective to attain and your chances of making up ground are wearing thin. Sometimes

you will be worrying about your opponent's score. You start thinking things like: 'If I get near the flag I'll gain one shot over my opponent', or, worse still, 'This shot needs to be absolutely faultless or it's going to take me three putts to get down'.

Minor faults in your chipping can be disastrous for your score. However skilled you are at technique, you should never forget the main principles of the swing: shift your body weight to the left, relax your forearms and use them only to control the head of your club.

Above **Imagine a little child sitting on the face of your club as you swing through.**

Right **Imagine a tee planted in the sand under the ball and try to break it with the blade of your sand wedge. If you are practising, you could even use a real tee to help you get underneath the ball.**

A brief reminder of the technique

Pitching

Use your sand wedge or pitching wedge when the sole purpose is to lift the ball and make it stop as quickly as possible on the green so that it does not roll on. You are most likely to use these clubs when there is an obstacle such as a bunker, a water hazard or a tree in front of the ball.

• Keep the face of your club open throughout the shot;
• The ball should be opposite your left heel;
• Open stance;
• Hands in front of the head of your club;
• Body weight slightly to the left;
• Shortened swing for a half-shot;
• You will need to make a divot if you are to create backspin.

Chip and run

Use a 7, 8 or 9 iron. Here the ball needs to go lower, but run more on the green, assuming there are no obstacles in the way. Use the club which is easiest to control.

• Ball midway between your feet;
• Open stance;
• Hands in front of the head of your club;
• Body weight slightly to the left;
• Less of a backswing;
• Don't make a divot;
• Don't use your wrists; use your hands, arms and shoulders to block the

shot as though you were playing a long putt;
• Keep the face of the club square throughout the shot;
• Judge the rhythm of the shot carefully;
• Keep your eye on the ball.

Exercises for sensory players

All the principles and exercises given above for the swing in general and bunker play in particular also apply to chipping.

Pay particular attention to your hands and feet. Your feet should feel the weight being transferred slightly to the left, and your hands should feel that there is proper contact with the

As far as possible, play the short game using your arms and shoulders, not your wrists. *Opposite page* This will be easier if you picture your arms and the line between your shoulders forming a triangle. This triangle does not change shape during the backswing or downswing.

ball. Keep your grip and your wrists firmer for chip-and-run shots than pitched ones.

If you want to be sure that your body weight is shifted to the left while you are practising, try crossing your legs at the address and when you play the shot.

Exercises for visual players

• A common mistake when playing chip-and-run shots is to break your wrists during the backswing or bring your right hand across your left in the downswing. A good way of correcting this is to imagine your shoulders and forearms as three sides of a triangle which stays the same shape all through the swing. This will also reduce the

Try chipping with your legs crossed to make sure you keep your weight to the left.

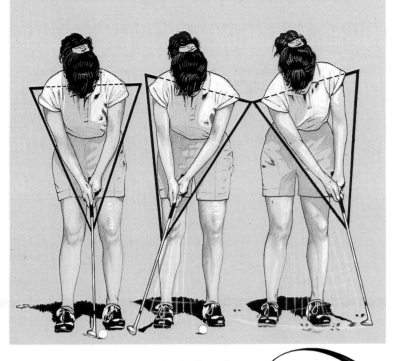

Below If there is a
hazard near the hole,
you will need to chip
so that the ball runs as
little as possible on the
green. Try imagining
the ball attached to a
parachute and
dropping gently onto
the green.

temptation to scoop up the ball and
drop it on the green.

• If you find that, no matter how hard
you try, you cannot stop yourself using
too much wrist action and this makes
you less accurate, you may like to think
of Ken Venturi with his forearms in
plaster to demonstrate his belief that
the short game is much more reliable if
you don't break your wrists. I once saw
him playing at his club at Eagle Creek,
Florida, and I can assure you he didn't
move them once!

• In a pitched shot, where it is essential
that the ball stops quickly on the green,
you might try imagining the ball attached to a parachute which lands it
neatly on the green.

117

Putting

• Using your brain

If you take 72 shots to go round an 18-hole golf course, roughly 36, or half your shots, will be putts. This figure shows how important putting is, but all too often it is an area neglected by golfers. This is also a part of the game where psychology is much more important than technique. Many professionals have failed to reach championship standard because their putting is weak; even top champions like Tom Watson have gone through some lengthy bad patches. Poor putting can easily cost you ten shots or more in a four-day event. Because the shot is so delicate, it is less easy to analyse whether you are playing it properly: instead of looking at the overall shot, you need to carry out a detailed analysis of mistakes which are difficult to spot. The best way of detecting an error is often by using images and sense impressions.

Another factor is that your fine musculature, which controls the small movements that putting requires, can very easily escape from your conscious control, especially if mental tension turns into muscle tension and distracts you from the messages your senses are sending you. So before talking about the proper technique and the psycho-logical exercises to help you, it is important to point out that there are many psychological variables which can affect your putting one way or the other.

Lack of confidence when putting can turn golf from a pleasure into a torment.

The need to succeed

The green is often your last chance: you *have* to succeed with your putt. It is possible to mis-hit a drive or an approach shot and yet sink a long putt for par, but not the opposite. It is all too easy for cold logic to take over from instinct on the green. This can turn into mental tension which makes you misread slopes and muscle tension which makes you less accurate. At its worst, tension can make your forearms go almost into spasm and stop you playing the shot altogether. The fear of missing combined with the need to succeed can make for an explosive mixture which needs to be dealt with by using positive antidotes.

Bad patches

Some putting problems are short-lived and can be spotted and corrected in a single practice session. If this does not happen, the bad patch may go on, with persistent tension leading to a growing lack of confidence. A similar thing sometimes happens in medicine: chronic stress can set off stomach secretions which in turn cause a stomach ulcer; the ulcer itself lasts long after the stress factors that caused it have disappeared. In this kind of situation, the green becomes a purgatory and the putter an instrument of torture. Some players try to exorcize their problems by acquiring new putters in the hope that this will solve the problem.

Positive motivation

The American psychologist Bob Rotella says putting can be fun. It is certainly true that you need to like putting if you are to succeed in golf. You need to be able to be completely convinced of exactly which line the ball is going to follow, concentrate on the target and think 'it's going to go in, it's going to go in'. Putting is the one area where positive thinking is most important, though you may be able to back up this thinking by relaxation or by using the systematic desensitization techniques described earlier in the book.

Michael Wolseley, formerly a Californian psychologist and now a golf pro in Paris, is well versed in these psychological techniques. When I met him recently at a Pro-Am, I saw him talking to the ball and suggesting to members of his team that they love their putt before playing the shot!

Your basic personality

The less important technique becomes, the more your own personality comes into play. If you are anxious, you will already be thinking about your putting before you get onto the green, often to the point where obsession with it affects other aspects of your game. If you are not confident in your putting ability, you will find yourself attacking the hole instead of carefully lining up for the centre of the green. Also, if you have an aggressive attitude towards the hole you may find yourself mis-hitting and ending up in a bunker.

If you plan your game properly, you will undoubtedly be thinking about your putting before arriving on the green, but in a positive way. You will be working out where you want the ball to land given the layout of the green and any obstacles that may exist.

But if you spend too much time planning your putts while on the green, you risk losing two penalty points for slow play, and are also likely to make yourself even more tense. It is worth noting that champion players think about the shot very carefully before they play it, but once they have lined everything up they complete the shot fairly quickly.

The voice of your unconscious

Personal factors will probably come into play in the way you putt; some people like to 'rattle the cup' while others prefer to let their ball 'die' into the hole. It goes without saying, of course, that you will not want to hit a downhill putt too hard. But you should always be aware of your deeper state of mind. As in technical ability, the difference between a good player and a champion is often virtually imperceptible. American Seniors professional Billy Casper rightly divides players into those who succeed in missing their putts and those who succeed in sinking their putts.

Michael Murphy says that when people in the first category say 'My putting's not going right', it means 'something's not going right at home, at work or in my unconscious'. So you need to read the situation in both the real and symbolic senses if you want to increase your chances of redeeming things.

● Technique

General principles

The stance, grip and position you use for putting are likely to be personal to you. There are plenty of books on the subject if you are unsure, but these are some of the fundamental principles:

● Some people (such as Seve Ballesteros) putt using their wrists; others (such as Lee Trevino and Bob Charles) use their arms, with their shoulders providing balance. Many players use a combination of the two.

● It is important to swing in the same three-speed sequence, even in putting.

● Putt by accelerating the club into the ball and try to play just past the hole (never up, never in!)

● Keep the face of your putter square as you hit the ball even allowing for the fact that some players' backswings are slightly out-to-in.

● Keep your eyes above the ball and don't move your head after hitting the ball.

Choosing a club

The putter is the club which shoulders the biggest weight of responsibility in golf. Some people prefer to stay faithful to one club; others prefer to change. People in the former category take comfort from using a single well-loved club; people in the second tend to stake everything on changing their putter as a way of dealing with problems in the way they play.

The technical aspects of choosing a putter are not vitally important. Some people prefer a heavy-headed club, especially where the greens are slow; others prefer a light club if the greens are fast. The colour, shape and blade size should all be what you feel most comfortable with. The one thing which is important is the shaft length, because this will be based on how far you bend over as you play. Some champion players, such as Johnny Miller, have tended to use very long putters adapted to their left forearm, which apparently makes it easier to putt in a straight line.

Reading the green

Here again, people tend to play using a combination of a small amount of technique and a large number of preconceptions. This applies especially to beginners, who have the habit of imitating top players they have seen on television. Since they cannot produce the same length of drive as the people they model themselves on, they imitate their relative slowness on the green. As some people have put it: if you're going to make a mess of it, make a mess of it quickly!

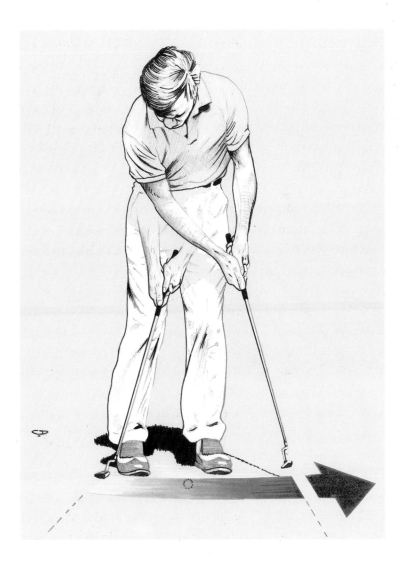

So check whether the grass has been cut recently and if so in which direction, but don't start getting down on your stomach with a magnifying glass to examine it!

Check the slope behind, in front of and to the sides of the ball. Even more usefully, watch which way your opponent putts if they play before you. If

Imagine the club passing through a yellow area into a red one to help you accelerate into the shot.

121

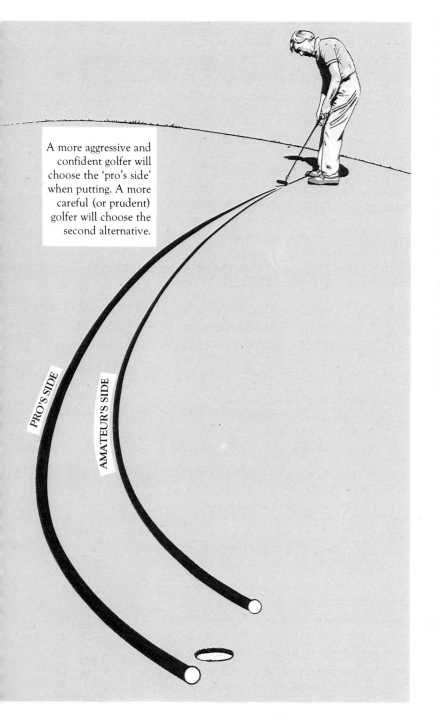

A more aggressive and confident golfer will choose the 'pro's side' when putting. A more careful (or prudent) golfer will choose the second alternative.

PRO'S SIDE

AMATEUR'S SIDE

you're still not sure, here is a good yardstick: eight times out of ten, the main slope of the green will follow that of the surrounding land. If this is the case, play from the side which is highest.

The slope of the green may affect your putting strategy. If there are two or more different gradients, the last one should determine the line of your putt because the ball will have lost some of its momentum by the time it reaches it. If you're a careful player, don't allow for too·much borrow; if the worst comes to the worst, play the shot and then if things go wrong you will have a second, uphill putt to play, which is easier. If you are playing more of an attacking game or are playing in competition, play as a professional would – with all the risks and benefits this entails.

● Advice from the champions

Golfing magazines provide plenty of advice from champions describing the way they play specific parts of the game. Here is some advice on the techniques and psychology of putting.

Ray Floyd advises looking straight at the ball, not the general area where it is lying. You might also imagine hitting a tack into the ball.

Frank Beard suggests hitting the logo on the ball.

Jose-Maria Olazabal says not to move your head until you hear the ball fall into the hole.

Johnny Miller and Jack Nicklaus both find it useful to bring their left elbow out (assuming you are a right-handed player).

Jack Nicklaus and Andy Bean both try to putt using a backswing as low as possible, just skimming the ground, rather than using the traditional image of a pendulum.

Tom Watson says don't change the angle of your elbows.

Craig Stadler suggests marking out a chalk line for the ball to follow – though only in practice, of course.

Bernhard Langer, who is well known for his periodic difficulties with putting, has partly solved his problems by breathing out as he hits the ball.

Sam Snead suggests lagging long putts and attacking short ones. In a long putt, the speed of the ball is rather more important than its direction. But for a short putt, precision and direction are more important than distance.

If all this advice is too much to absorb, at least remember the following two points, because they encapsulate all the others:

● Use the three-stage rhythm of the swing when you putt.
● Try to hit the ball in a solid, yet fluid way. Your practice swing should be closer to a caress than a knock.

● Exercises for sensory players

In the first half of this book, we looked at how the way you perceive life affects the way you learn golf. If you rely more on feelings, Timothy Gallwey's book *The Inner Game of Golf* should be your bible. If you are more of a visual player, try the following advice.

● To find out what a shot should feel like, work on it first without your club and then without the ball. Try to notice the different feelings you get from the grip and the interaction between your hands. You may find it feels better to keep the palms of your hands turned outwards at 45°.

stopped short or long. Now open your eyes and see whether your feelings were correct.

Keeping your eyes shut is very useful, but also very frustrating. It is a telling demonstration of the limitations of the left-hand side of your brain, which you use all through your life. At least seven times out of ten, the shots you play with your eyes closed will be more accurate.

• Another way of improving the sensory feedback you receive when putting is to use your driver instead of your putter. This is also very useful (if, again, somewhat frustrating), since it teaches you how to swing into the ball rather than just hitting it.

Finally, Michel Damiano suggests a good exercise: if you want to explore the feelings you get from your right hand, which has a tendency to domi-

One good exercise is to keep your head still and stare at the hole instead of the ball as you begin your putt.

• Tension often makes you grip the club too tightly. Try out the two extremes, with and without the ball: first by holding it very tightly, and then very loosely. Work out which is closer to your normal style of putting.

• Play several putts and rate them on a scale of one to five depending on the amount of tension in your hands, with five as the maximum and one as the minimum. Which figure do you feel most at ease with? Try repeating the exercise with your eyes shut.

• Line up as though to play a normal putt, then close your eyes and play it. Before you open your eyes, try to work out whether the ball is to the right or left of the target, and whether it has

nate your left, keep it very high, on your left forearm rather than the grip. This will also enable you to feel the sensations you get from your left arm, which should help you to hit the ball in a straight line.

• Exercises for visual players

If you prefer to use visual feedback or mental images, or a combination of the two, try the following.

Visual feedback
• Try putting in front of a mirror: look at your stance, the way the head of the putter moves, whether you keep your body still, and so on.
• Use intermediate targets along the line of your putt. Better still, divide the ball-to-hole line into equal parts.
• To help you play the ball past the hole, put a visible object, such as a bottle, immediately beyond the hole and try to hit it.
• Bob Toski suggests visualizing the ball-to-hole line. Before you play your putt, try a practice shot, and follow the line of the imaginary ball with your eyes, at the same speed as the ball would travel.

Images
Using mental images is one of the most effective ways of improving your putting because it means you can replace a mechanical method with a psychological approach.

• If the green is very fast, or particularly slow and wet, instead of hitting the ball harder or less hard, try imagining that the hole is closer or further away than it really is.
• If you find it hard to play straight

Left Many coaches suggest making your putting more accurate by aiming at a smaller target such as a coin, a tee or another ball.

Below A good putt should always be aimed just past the hole. Try playing towards a real or imaginary obstacle, such as a bottle, immediately behind the hole.

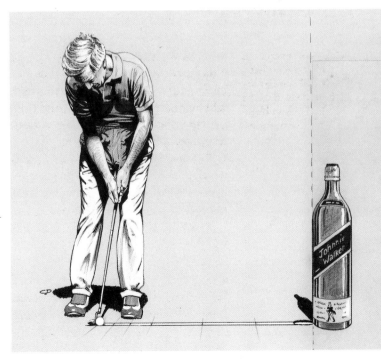

Imagine that the hole is nearer than it really is when putting downhill, and further away when putting uphill.

It is important to be able to shut yourself off from visual distractions and noise when putting.

If you have trouble putting straight, don't try pushing the ball towards the hole: imagine a vacuum cleaner sucking it into the hole.

because you tend to push the ball, try imagining that you are not pushing, but pulling the putter and the ball towards the hole. Golf Digest suggests that you imagine pulling a toy lorry along on a piece of string.

My own particular favourite is the image of the ball being sucked straight into the hole by a vacuum cleaner, or perhaps attached to the hole by a piece of elastic.

• Picture the hole as a cave or tunnel which makes you want to go in, perhaps with a warm, welcoming light inside.

• Imagine that the line the ball is to follow is a magnetic track.

• Pretend you are surrounded by a glass dome which prevents you from being distracted by outside noise.

• Perhaps the most effective technique of all, whether you are a visual or a sensory player, is to imagine the hole

much larger than it is, perhaps getting bigger, and decide what feelings this causes in you.

PLAYING GOLF

The Psychology of Practice

• Why practise?

No professional would ever ask themselves this question: practice is an integral part of any sport as highly competitive as golf. If you are an amateur golfer, perhaps playing only at weekends, you are likely to have limited leisure time available and there will be a temptation to skimp on practice in favour of more games. But practice is essential if you are to build on what you have learned and acquire new skills. If you have mastered the principles of the swing, for example, you will find it is much easier to regain this skill after a break, though it may take several sessions to regain your skills in the short game.

Practice needs to be approached in a positive frame of mind, because it is not going to work unless you want to do it in the first place and you feel good about it afterwards. One friend of mine only goes to the driving range as a way of punishing himself after a particularly bad game. Practice becomes a form of atonement for his sins. All he does when he practises is to repeat all the same bad habits which had led him to make mistakes on the golf course.

There are also other motives at work on the driving range, since this is a better place than a golf course when it comes to flaunting your golfing prowess. We have already shown how it is easier to show off in a game like tennis, which takes place on a limited territory. The driving range may be a good place to meet people, but there is also a tendency to concentrate on the shots you are best at so as to impress your audience.

Practice can also satisfy the psychological quest for perfection. When I used to go sailing, I was always surprised at how some people preferred to spend their time polishing their brasswork or cleaning their decks rather than actually going out sailing. The same kind of thing happens in golf, where people are more fanatical about practising than they are about playing, and may be perfectly good at demonstrating swing techniques but useless when it comes to playing a real game.

Practice should also be a form of

leisure and relaxation in just the same way as other people go jogging. When I was a guest lecturer at Montreal University, I was delighted to see that there were four or five students who used to come along to my lectures with golf bags, which they would leave in the cloakroom outside. As soon as they had an hour of free time, they would dash off to the university golf range to play a few dozen balls before the next lecture.

Although many of the reasons for practice are the same as those for playing, there is always the danger of confusing the ultimate objective. You should never be trying to improve your swing and make a good impression at the same time.

Practice sessions should be spent not only working on your technical weaknesses, but also setting yourself positive psychological goals. Try out some of the hundred or more suggestions in this book and adopt the ones that suit you best. Don't simply take everything on board uncritically: try each technique out, and either accept or reject it.

● How to make your practice interesting

We have already emphasized the importance of being positively motivated when you practise. The best way of doing this is to set yourself specific objectives and to vary these so that they are always interesting.

Setting yourself goals

One of the basic principles of education is that you can't learn two new things at the same time, especially if they contradict each other. In golf, the best way to set goals is to have an indirect objective. For example, if you want to learn to hit the ball higher you could work on leg play. This means that the left-hand side of your brain is involved in planning the exercise, but the right-hand side actually carries it out.

This objective may either be a technical or a psychological one, as long as it is clearly defined and varied. If you go on obstinately and mechanically repeating an exercise you will not achieve any progress, no matter how long you do it.

Peter Crandford's *The Winning Touch in Golf* gives some interesting pointers to success. For putting practice, he suggests scattering balls around the hole, so as to reproduce conditions out on the course. This is better and more fun than doing the same thing time and again. An alternative solution is more time-consuming, but has the distinct psychological advantage in that it combines chipping and putting.

Crandford suggests that you take nine good balls, and chip shots up to the nearest hole, then continue putting. Try eighteen in all, varying the distance from the hole each time. It is surprising how easy the chips seem and how many of the putts prove difficult. Crandford believes that a combination of chipping and putting is the fastest

method of keeping the number of strokes down. And it is also a good way of preventing your game from deteriorating if you do not have time for a complete round often enough.

He also gives some hints on driving with a wooden club. Given that a standard 18-hole golf course usually needs about 14 drives, Crandford says you should try and keep score during practice on how many successive drives would be playable. When you reach the stage where you are getting 14 good drives in succession, you know you won't be wasting too many shots off the tee.

Some driving ranges are specifically designed as practice courses, and contain all the different situations you are likely to come across on a golf course.

This has the dual advantage of improving your game and being enjoyable.

● Psychological errors to avoid

Confusing quality with quantity

Try to attain excellence through quality rather than quantity. If your practice sessions are too long and tiring, they will make you more tense and more likely to keep making the same mistakes. Overdoing your practice can lead to a similar problem to that which occurs if you practise too hard immediately before a competition: venting excess energy instead of warming up for the sensations you will feel when playing in competition.

Pointless repetition

There was one golfer I knew who was lucky enough to have a great deal of spare time in the afternoons and would therefore spend them on the course. This was unsatisfactory because he had problems with his short game and his putting. In practice sessions, he spent far too long on the green because he assumed that the best way to improve his game was to keep on imitating champion golfers he had seen on television. But his problem was less one of technique than tension, and he was totally out of touch with the messages his muscles and sensations were giving him.

Avoiding negative habits

The best way to enjoy a meal in a restaurant is to stop eating when you still have some room left. This also applies to golf: too much practice can give you indigestion. If necessary, cancel a practice session if you don't feel well or you simply don't feel like it. Vary your practice, and if you still can't play a shot properly, don't stick at it obstinately: give your 'muscular memory' time to absorb what you have learned. Finally, if you decide that a practice session isn't getting you anywhere, then stop.

● Problem holes

Gary Wiren suggests practising in the same conditions as that of the game itself. Bob Toski used to write the names of his opponents, people like Snead and Hogan, on his golf balls. If there are specific holes that you have major problems with (nemesis holes), concentrate on them. The 9th hole on the red course at Rabat in Morocco is a par 3 surrounded by water, which has wrought havoc with many a professional's score. One player lost four or five balls in the water, and finally his partner asked with heavy irony whether he was trying to build a bridge out of balls so that he could cross without getting his feet wet!

What to do between practice sessions

One very important aid to practice is a diary. It has the following advantages:

● Monitoring the effectiveness of your practice;
● Providing a written record of the skills you have learned;
● Giving you the enjoyment of working out scores, calculating averages, perhaps even drawing graphs.

Another more unusual way of taking notes is to use a scorecard to list the mistakes you make during a practice game. Note down things like mis-hits, problems with distance and direction, shots played too quickly and mistakes caused by muscular tension.

Left Scorecard

PLAYER	HOLE NO.	DISTANCE	MEN'S PAR	Notes
81	TOT	6555	72	
40	OUT	3300	36	
41	IN	3255	36	
5	18	500	5	Still putting right
4	17	180	3	Didn't complete routine on 2nd putt
5	16	355	4	Not enough club – tried to hit hard and went into water
4	15	350	4	Pitch shot short – allowing for too much run
5	14	495	5	Pushing putts or leaving short – too much run
4	13	330	4	Into grain on putt – left it short
6	12	470	4	Tried to hit it too hard – froze
4	11	200	3	Wind again – this time short – got to think better
4	10	375	4	O.K.
40	OUT	3300	36	
4	9	404	4	Better iron shot
3	8	166	3	Pulled iron here – overreacted to last iron shot
4	7	416	4	Another pushed iron – fighting hook thoughts
5	6	485	5	Pulled my putt – afraid would miss it right
4	5	184	3	Too much club. Didn't allow for wind
7	4	490	5	Wind left to right made me tight – blocked
3	3	340	4	Good mental image
5	2	415	4	Negative thought on iron shot – thinking hook
5	1	400	4	Didn't warm up – not ready

Legend

|	Straight shot
	Pull
/	Push
	Hook
	Slice
T	Short
↑	Long
s	Sand
w	Water
o	Out-of-bounds

DATE ___ SCORE ___ WITNESSED BY ___

Right Scorecard

HOLE NO.	DISTANCE	MEN'S PAR	PLAYER	DRIVE	2ND SHOT	3RD SHOT	PUTTS
TOT	6555	72	81				
OUT	3300	36	40				
IN	3255	36	41				
18	500	5	5		T	T	/
17	180	3	4	/			↑T 3
16	355	4	5	—	Tw	/	20 1
15	350	4	4	—	✓	T	10 1
14	495	5	5	—	/	—	/2
13	330	4	4	/	—	T	T 2
12	470	4	6	o	—	/	/2
11	200	3	4	T	←		T 2
10	375	4	4	T	—		T 2
OUT	3300	36	40				
9	404	4	4				/2
8	166	3	3		Ts		15 1
7	416	4	4	—	T	T	5 1
6	485	5	5	—	—		2
5	184	3	4	←			↑/3
4	490	5	7	o	T	Ts	/2
3	340	4	3	/	—		7 1
2	415	4	5	—	T	T	2
1	400	4	5	—			/2

The card opposite is reproduced from Gary Wiren's *The New Golf Mind*. The top half of the card shows the player's psychological mistakes, and the lower half gives a more detailed profile of what happened during the round.

If you own a computer, you might use it to store your practice programmes and competition results. There is something nice about the idea of applying late-twentieth century technology to the time-honoured traditions of golf. If you analyse your performance in this way, you can then tailor your practice schedules accordingly: this is a good way of using the analytical left-hand side of your brain and keeping the right hemisphere for the game itself.

● Out-of-season practice

Winter nets

In bad winter weather, you will often not have the ability or inclination to play golf, either on a driving range or on the course itself. Many golfers therefore set up nets in their gardens or garages so that they can practise their swing all year round. This is often a good idea, though not as effective as practice on a golf range. You have no visual feedback about the success or otherwise of your shots, unless another golfer is there with you or you can record your swing on video.

More likely, you will need to make do with keeping in trim physically and practise your 'muscular memory' in the swing. This type of practice will be more effective if you use feelings and images: put the emphasis on the lightness of the ball, feeling the weight of the club, how fast you play the shot, and so on.

Indoor putting

The traditional cartoon image of golfers who secretly practise their putts on the office carpet with a 'do not disturb' sign hanging on the door is not always that far from the truth. Many a husband, wife or secretary will tell you that indoor putting practice is much more common than you might think. Practising like this has obvious advantages, provided you apply the principles of learning through psycho-golf: keep your practice varied and interesting, and set yourself objectives in terms of the direction and length of your putts. And don't forget that the conditions on your office carpet are not quite the same as on a rainy, windswept golf course . . .

Keeping in condition

Not all golf champions have the physique of an athlete, and this has given rise to the misconception that golf is not a 'real' sport like tennis or football. But although it may place less of a load on your heart and lungs, your frame and muscles come in for a hard time when you play golf. Running should

form an integral part of your practice, especially in winter when the weather makes playing golf more difficult. Fitness training or even just press-ups in the morning should help you to stay in trim and recover your condition more quickly when you start playing golf again in the spring.

On the Course

● Your state of mind

After you have taken your first lessons on the driving range and made your début on the golf course, you may well be disappointed by your performance. Although you have passed the first hurdle in your golfing career, the next ones seem higher. Practice on the driving range concentrates on the swing: now you have to learn to judge distances and the layout of the course and deal with natural obstacles. Learning these skills is a slow, gradual process.

During this time, your state of mind is likely to oscillate between fear and self-doubt on the one hand, and over-confidence on the other. Over-confidence will tempt you to play shots that are too risky for your level of experience. So any pro worth their salt will give you as much practice in the psychology of golf as in its techniques, with the emphasis on positive thinking.

Many learners have an almost superstitious attitude to their equipment. Apart from the justifiable phobia about long irons which many beginners suffer from, you will often hear young golfers saying things like: 'My 8 iron is my favourite club', or 'I always have to play my approach shots with a pitching wedge because I don't feel comfortable with my sand wedge'.

As a more experienced player who has already played in competition, one of the most important skills to learn is that of playing single-mindedly, without being distracted by other players. Whether your partner never opens their mouth or prattles away non-stop, both can interfere with your game. Also, consciously or unconsciously imitating their swing can have a good or bad effect on your own game. Another skill that takes some learning is getting on with the game without worrying about what you regard as being 'problem' holes. Just because your ball went in the water on the 4th hole last time round doesn't mean it's going to happen again.

Another problem for experienced golfers is playing matches away from your usual territory. The psychological tension caused by the fact that you never know what is round the next corner can ruin your swing.

In all these situations, the state of mind that is going to do you the most good is one of confidence in yourself and your abilities. If you are sufficiently confident, there is no reason why you should not play an unfamiliar course just as well as your own home course.

• Minimizing risk

A good golf course should be designed with the hazards placed so that they will penalize bad shots. For example, a water hazard to the right of centre 170 yards from the tee will be the punishment for a heavily sliced drive.

A good course will also penalize players who take too many risks. This is often the case with courses designed by Peter Dye, where the par 5 holes can be reached in two, but at a very high degree of risk. In most cases you should make a realistic assessment of the situation, depending on whether you are playing an attacking game or a more defensive one, and then aim to play holes like these in par rather than going for a birdie.

The psychological goals you should aim to achieve are these:

Staying in the comfort zone
All players have a comfort zone in which they feel at ease. This space is both a technical and psychological one, and is broadly reflected in your handicap. The size of this comfort zone will be reduced if you are aiming for too low a score, playing with new partners or on a course which is unfamiliar to you or has a reputation for difficulty.

Assessing risks properly
I have always wondered why it is that people who are perfectly capable of analysing risks all day long at work, and well able to take complex surgical decisions in a hospital or financial decisions in a bank, don't seem to bother with this elementary precaution when it comes to playing golf. Most likely, the problem is that they have total faith in their own abilities and their motives for playing golf. Going round a golf course should be a constant process of assessing risk and setting yourself achievable goals.

Bob Toski suggests playing golf with the addition of a new rule: every time you force your drive into a clump of trees, drop the ball on the fairway 15 yards back from where it should be. In the long term, this will gain you shots rather than losing them!

Accepting the inevitability of mistakes
In the medical profession we accept that with all diseases, whether they be rheumatism, heart disease or cancer, some of our patients will be cured and some of them will die. But we are often involved with cases which fall into neither category, and here we have to determine the margins of risk or error involved, and the advantages and disadvantages of treatment we give to the patient. For example, it is generally agreed that chemotherapy is necessary because it can save the patient's life, even though its toxicity can cause a major deterioration in the quality of their life in terms of hair loss, nausea and so on.

I think that the best psychological attitude to adopt in any situation, including a game of golf, is that of mak-

ing the best of things as they are. Everyone makes mistakes, and if you're feeling that nothing can go wrong as you play, that feeling is likely to be short-lived.

● Don't set yourself too many objectives

Many golfing books tend to overload you with information and expect you to take on board far more than the human brain is capable of dealing with. There is a common tendency to forget that there's more than one way of attaining the same objective: for example, two people can swing in two different ways and still play a shot which reaches the target. Over the history of golf, there have been many different schools of thought about whether to play the swing with the arms or legs, or whether to chip with the wrists firm (Ken Venturi) or flexible (Seve Ballesteros). It is important to understand these different theories, but it is also important to forget them when it comes to playing the shot. If you're playing a chip and trying to think about the length of the shot, the trajectory of the ball, keeping an open stance with your weight on your left foot, shifting your weight, keeping your right elbow close to your body, making sure your head is behind the ball, steering the club with your left hand and hitting the ball with your right, you are going to be a nervous

wreck by the time you get round to playing the shot. It is much better to have a single idea in your mind, if possible in the form of an image or feeling, than to have a long checklist to go through before you play.

● Reducing unnecessary variables

This is one of the simplest and most effective ways of achieving progress. It is beautifully expressed by Peter Crandford in his book, *The Winning Touch in Golf.* Just as scientists reduce the number of variables to make sure that their results are as accurate as possible, so Crandford says the same principle can be applied to golf. He describes the hypothetical situation of a robot player built to look like a human. When the robot is tried out for the first time, it mis-hits shots, so its inventors decide to tighten up some parts of it. For example, the top half of the robot sways around too much when it plays, so they bolt its head so that it cannot move. By doing this they have eliminated one variable: the robot's head is fixed in one position. Then the scientists find that the lower half of the body is not planted squarely enough on the ground. So they eliminate this variable by tightening up the screw fastening the robot to the ground so that its feet are more in control of its movements. Finally, they find that the club swivels in the robot's hands as it hits the ball. So they remove this variable by welding the robot's hands to the shaft of the club.

Try to eliminate as many variables in your game as possible, so that you have a clear idea of what will happen if you play a particular shot. If you are not sure which technique to use in a particular situation, choose the one which involves the fewest variables. If you want to play a hook to the left, you have a choice between closing the face of your club, closing your stance, or accentuating the movement of your right hand. The best solution is to close the face of your club because it involves the least change and the fewest variables.

You can also apply this principle to your short game. If you want to play different types of running shot, you can either choose a different club (a 7, 8 or 9 iron) or you can use the same club but with different movements. Whichever you opt for, you should not use both variables at the same time.

● Before you tee off

It is important to get rid of anything which might cause you more tension than necessary. This means reducing the number of imponderables as you prepare for the game. You can do this by not arriving at the last minute, not

Anxiety at the tee-off can easily assume nightmare proportions.

playing shots you're not used to, and not changing putters even though you may have had a bad time on the greens the day before! Anything unexpected or unplanned is bound to make you more tense.

Keep your mind alert and determined, but clear and calm as well. Timothy Gallwey says: 'Imagine that the mind is like a lake. When its surface is calm, reflections of trees, clouds, birds, etc. can be seen clearly and in rich detail, as can whatever is in its depths. But when the surface is ruffled by the wind, it does not reflect clearly. Objects look darker, less distinct, even distorted. Likewise, the mind that is restless or agitated cannot make clear contact with reality, and then we have a difficult time dealing with our surroundings. Hence quietening the mind is the first step to the first level of concentration.'

Another problem is that when you tee off at the first hole, your mind is probably still on the last thing you did: how you got to the course, what you were doing at the office before you left. The best way to avoid this is to have a brief warm-up session before you start playing: this may be either physical or psychological. Many pros recommend stretching exercises specially designed for golf, to help you rotate your shoulders and free up your spinal column. Other golfers prefer practising a few shots using two clubs at the same time, and then playing them with one club to give them the feeling of lightness. Another alternative is breathing: if you are tense, you are likely to be inhaling more deeply than you exhale, and you will therefore be short of breath and have hunched shoulders. If you breathe out more strongly by breathing from your stomach instead of your lungs, this will almost certainly make you more relaxed.

If you get the chance to go and sit under a tree on your own for a few moments before the game, try shutting your eyes and deciding which parts of your body feel most tense. Try tuning in to the noises and smells around you, and when you have done this, visualize the first hole. In the words of Johnny Miller, you should check your pressure in the same way as you do with the tyres of your car. Too much or too little pressure can be dangerous.

If you do try a couple of practice swings without the ball, don't use this as a last-minute opportunity to work on your technique: just try and find the movement that feels most comfortable. If you practise your putting, play a few strokes without any particular aim in mind, simply to relax your muscles, and then try setting yourself a few easy-to-achieve targets.

The most distracting thought that can occur before you tee off is that other people are watching you, whether it is simply your fellow players or an audience. The best cure for this fear is simply to play the game in your own way for your benefit, not anybody else's.

● Before you play a shot

Posture

Here we are talking not about the techniques of the address and stance, but your psychological posture. This should be one of *active relaxation*. Perhaps the best comparison is with a cat poised to spring: although it is concentrating very intensely, its muscles are sufficiently relaxed for it to jump well. Athletes who need to build up speed, such as long-jumpers or sprinters, will be familiar with the idea of active relaxation. In golf, this should be concentrated in your hands and feet, because between them they control the rest of the shot.

If you feel that your body weight is well distributed and your feet firmly planted on the ground and facing slightly inwards, with your legs in the form of an X, you are bound to feel confident. Keep your grip light but firm, and if in doubt clench your left hand slightly more tightly than your right.

It is very easy to forget to relax your arms, especially your left forearm. This is likely to be because you have misinterpreted the instruction to keep your left arm straight – but straight does not necessarily mean tense.

Practice swings

Most golfers play a practice swing; more experienced players tend to play a half-shot which gives them an idea of the feelings they want to experience. This is the waggle: small movements of the hands and club which help the wrists to relax. If you are less sure of yourself, play a whole swing, preferably as hard as you would a real one. If you repeat this two or three times it should help you to reduce your anxiety as you actually hit the ball.

Practice swings serve more of a psychological than a physical purpose by eliminating tension and making you feel more decisive. They are more important for your short game, where if you try out the shot first it will give you an idea of what size of stroke you have to play in relation to the distance the ball has to travel.

If you find yourself playing a very hard practice shot, it is because you are trying too hard. This is a very common feature of many people's golf. Timothy Gallwey has described what he calls the five different ways of trying too hard:

- Trying to *hit* the ball instead of swinging into it.
- Trying to hit the ball up into the air.
- Trying to hit the ball a long way: this puts too much emphasis on your muscles and not enough on your brain.
- Trying to hit the ball *straight*: the closer you get to the pin, the more afraid you are of missing.
- Trying to hit the ball 'right'. If you spend too much time dissecting your swing and analysing it in purely

Free up your hands before you start the swing, but don't forget to make sure your forearms are relaxed. Hold your left arm straight, but not absolutely rigid.

mechanical terms, the chances are that you will develop an overly self-critical attitude and forget that where golfing technique is concerned, the whole is more than the sum of the parts.

● Using your mind during the swing

At first sight, the swing seems to go against the dictates of logic. The harder you try to hit the ball, the less far it seems to go, and the higher you want it to go, the more you have to hit it downwards!

One way of coming to terms with the latter is to use a mental image. If you take your club and hit the ground with it, it will bounce. If you throw the club in front of you, it will slide along the ground instead of bouncing. Newton's third law of motion says that to every action there is an equal and opposite reaction. If you bring the club down onto the ball and create a divot, the ball will tend to rise, but if you deliberately try to lift it off the ground, you will be using your arms too much and end up with a low or topped shot.

Use the principles of psycho-golf during your swing by remembering a single idea about technique, such as 'Shift your weight during the downswing'. Better still, think about something indirect, such as your breathing and muscle tension, or visualize the target you are trying to reach. Some people prefer to think in visual terms of the shot they want to play; others prefer gestalt-type images: playing inside a barrel, finishing with their hands in the clouds or hitting the ball as though they were slamming a door. Any of these images could help you relax during your swing.

Some players are actually able to empty their minds during the half-minute or so before they play a shot. Many golf courses are situated near airports because the land is cheap and other forms of building are impossible due to aircraft noise. Many people playing at Doral, near Miami airport, eventually stop noticing the noise of the jets passing overhead.

When you have finished your swing, there is a strong temptation to raise your head to see where the ball has gone. This has the effect of shifting one of the two fixed points on which the shot is centred. If you move your head, it is very hard to play a stable swing. The best way to deal with this is to con-centrate on watching your club hit the ball, rather than not moving your head, since your brain is more likely to respond to positive instructions than negative ones.

● Between shots

Most golfers lose more strokes in between shots than they do by misjudging their swing, simply because they spend this time thinking. Every golfer knows that it is very hard to put a bad shot or a difficult hole out of your mind, and sometimes it can ruin the whole day's golf.

It is easy to underestimate the psychological importance of the period between shots: this is why, if you play a long and intensive session on a golf range, you often emerge mentally and physically exhausted. There are many benefits to be gained from walking between shots:

● If the right-hand side of your brain is over-occupied with anxiety about the way the game is going, contemplation of nature and the use of your senses of sight, hearing and smell will distract it from these worries.
● If you do count sheep or find a similar way of taking your mind off things, this will tend to prevent the analytical left-hand side of your brain from planning how you are going to play the next shot. This is particularly important in combating slow play, which can make you less motivated and more tense.

• Talking to your fellow-players can be very good for you. Apart from important competitions and match play, I think that a certain amount of conversation and socialization are an essential part of golf. If your partner goes round the course without uttering a single word, I think they have probably chosen the wrong sport. Having said that, there is nothing worse than a complicated business conversation for putting you off your stride. Worst of all is the situation where someone invites you out for a game and then uses it as an excuse for a free four-hour consultation!

• Walking between shots helps you to establish an emotional relationship with the course; some players prefer a master–servant relationship with the course, while others like to make friends with it. When you come to what you regard as an 'unlucky hole', walking gives you the chance to decide whether it is still an unlucky hole or whether you might be able to come to some sort of amicable arrangement with it.

• Finally, it is between shots that you are most likely to start getting obsessed with your score. Sometimes this may be caused by failure to play to your handicap; at others, it may be that you are worried at just how well you are playing. This is why some players regularly crack up at the last three holes: it has nothing to do with whether they are tired or not.

Thinking about your score as you play stops you from concentrating on what you are doing now and makes you more likely to set yourself over-ambitious objectives so as to catch up. Peter Crandford likens a good game of golf to making a pearl necklace. He says that each good shot is a precious pearl which has its own value: you can only create one at a time, so you shouldn't be concerned by the ones you've already made or the ones you still have to make. If you give each pearl the same amount of concentration, the necklace as a whole will be a thing of beauty.

Playing in Competition

● Preparing for competition

• Use a countdown before the match. If you tee off at 11 a.m., be at the golf course at 10 o'clock, an hour early. If it takes you half an hour to get to the course, leave home promptly at 9.30; if it takes you an hour to get ready, get up at 8.30.

• Never hurry or try to do too much as you prepare for the game, so that you are in full possession of your faculties when you start playing.

• Another must is a good breakfast. You will be expending a considerable amount of energy over the space of four hours or more. Even if you don't normally have breakfast or you're not hungry, make the effort to have a proper breakfast of fruit juice, cereal, bacon and eggs or something similar. Take some dried fruit or something sugary with you to eat as you go round the course; if your energy level wanes at all, it could lose you the match. Have some water to drink every couple of holes, especially if the weather is hot.

• Wear clothes that you feel comfortable in. Don't forget an extra pullover in case it gets cold, and wear comfortable

shoes, since you are going to be walking more than 5 miles.

• Assuming you arrive at the clubhouse at 10 o'clock, don't spend hours chatting to your friends; start to prepare yourself mentally before you go into the changing room or register for the match. This should take you up until about 10.20; then have a practice session, since it is essential that you warm up before any game. Start with a few exercises to loosen you up, and then take a wedge or a 9 iron and play a few short strokes. Gradually increase the length of the shots using more powerful clubs and ending with your driver. Don't spent more than 20 minutes practising: the aim is to loosen up your body and warm up your muscles before the competition, not to fine-tune your swing.

Now you have a quarter of an hour before you are due to start. Go to the putting green, take three or four balls and start with some very short putts of 12 to 16 inches. At this kind of distance you should be able to sink them; the sound of a golf ball falling into the hole is an excellent confidence-booster at this stage. Finally, play a few long putts to get a feel for hitting the ball. And now it's time to go to the first tee. Good luck!

● On the course

Be positive. As Arnold Palmer once put it, if you don't attack the course, it'll attack you. You know your own skills and abilities: try to make full use of them. Never play beyond your capabilities, and don't try to play impossible shots. Think carefully about the type of shot you are going to play, the weather conditions and the state of the greens. In other words, concentrate; but try to empty your mind after the first shot by enjoying your natural surroundings, looking at the trees and listening to the birds. Then turn your mind back to the match before you arrive at the ball to play your second shot. Don't keep up a constant level of pressure for the whole game, or you risk collapsing under the strain before the 18th green! When you have taken a decision, stick to it: there is nothing worse than having last-minute doubts as you line up to play the shot you have planned, whether it be a long drive or a short putt. Don't let yourself be distracted by your opponents, and don't be too chatty. Here again, this will vary according to your own tastes: there are some people, like South Africa's Bobby Locke (four times winner of the British Open), who will shake your hand at the beginning of the match and apologize that they will not be uttering a single word for the next four hours. There are also people like Lee Trevino, who often keeps up a steady stream of wisecracks all through the game. But you must be able to concentrate constantly, and lack of conversation is a small price to pay for success.

● Attacking or defensive golf

It goes without saying that you must have a positive attitude if you want to get a good score. You will get birdies if you attack the pin with approach shots and putts. At the same time, footballers who play in defence tend not to score goals.

A great deal will depend on the following factors:

● The rules of the particular competition;
● Your position after two rounds;
● The whereabouts of the pin on the green;
● Your own personality.

Your game will also be different depending on whether you are in a matchplay or medal play tournament. In matchplay, you should adapt your style of play to your opponent's results; if they are winning, you should start taking more risks to try and get ahead again, but if you're ahead, you should be much more cautious.

In medal play, you are playing against everyone else, and should therefore have a more cautious attitude: only take risks if they are worth it.

In a four-round tournament, if you

are not leading after the third round but victory is still within sight, you will need to play more aggressively if you are to achieve a high placing or even win.

On the fourth round of a tournament, the tournament committee tends to take a perverse pleasure in placing the pins on the most inaccessible parts of the greens to make the course as hard as possible: behind a bunker or water hazard, or almost out of bounds. In cases like these, playing to the pin is a very high-risk process which requires a huge amount of self-discipline and total confidence in your game. Personally, I don't think twice about going for the hole if I'm playing a 6 or 7 iron; from that distance I'm quite happy to get the ball onto the middle of the green.

Everybody has different ways of playing in situations like these. People like Seve Ballesteros, Greg Norman and Sandy Lyle take many more risks than, say, Tom Watson or Jack Nicklaus, who are much more solid, reliable players.

• The role of superstition

Golf is such a delicate and difficult game that there are sometimes moments when the smallest unexpected event can throw you off track, ruin your swing and have you wishing the rest of the tournament was cancelled. In cases like this, where such a setback can send you into a crisis of despair, it is very common to seize on anything which offers the faintest glimmer of hope. Many players will use a new ball if they feel the old one is letting them down; others have much more elaborate and complex systems of superstition.

One well-known professional always stands on the same side of the tee while awaiting his turn to tee off. Another common superstition is to use the same ball as the previous day if you feel it brought you luck then.

The fact that some top players are superstitious shows that this kind of ritual can provide a valuable boost to your confidence provided you don't become obsessed by it.

Golf and its Players

● Seniors

Golf players become seniors at the age of 50. It is always worth watching the great names of the European and American circuits playing in seniors tournaments. They include names like:

● Chichi Rodriguez, who still goes round the course smiling and singing and is still one of the most agile players around;
● Australia's Bruce Crampton, solitary and hard-up;
● Bob Toski, one of the greatest of all coaches, who now says he plans to take part only in senior tours;
● Peter Thompson, the undisputed master in the 1960s, with four British Open wins to his credit;
● Gary Player, with his iron muscles, still in quest of perfection;
● Georges Bayer, 6′ 6″ tall, once one of the world's most powerful players;
● Doug Sanders, still the picture of elegance, with his matching pastel blue shoes, gloves, umbrella, pullover and trousers.

The roll of honour includes many other leading names: Billy Casper, Sam Snead, Harold Henning and Roberto de Vicenzo are all playing competitive golf just as they did in their prime.

It is interesting to watch their technique, and see how this has inevitably changed over the years. The backswing tends to come up only to the right shoulder, since their bodies are not as supple as they used to be, and they have to hit the ball much harder to achieve a good distance. They also tend to use lighter clubs and make more use of their hands to accelerate the head of the club on impact. If anything, seniors put in more practice than younger players, though with more emphasis on improving their accuracy in the short game (chipping, pitching and putting). They are aware that they are going to become less strong as they grow older, and intensive short game practice is much more testing. Seniors tend to stop concentrating on their swing on the grounds that they are not going to be able to improve it, but there is still plenty of room for improvement in their putting.

● Women

Golf has come a long way since the early days of British golf, when many courses would not allow women to play on certain days of the week. Nowadays, women golfers are in most respects equal to men. They also have many advantages, especially psychological ones, over men.

Women taking up golf for the first time are much better learners because they are more attentive and disciplined than men, and they do not need to display their masculinity by hitting the ball as hard as possible. Men tend to get disappointed when they mis-hit and be too impatient to correct problems because this slows them down in their quest for greater performance. Often, a woman player will make up for her lack of distance by being more skilled in her short game. Because women put less aggression and more enjoyment into the game, they tend not to get as rattled as men do when things go wrong. They are also more likely to use relaxation techniques, such as meditation or yoga, before they play important games.

In many ways, male golf players have a great deal to learn from their female counterparts, and women have compensated for their technical disadvantages by developing other more psychological skills.

• Juniors

I have lost count of the number of times I have heard people saying they're going to take up golf when they get older and can't play tennis any longer. The problem is that a few years later these very same people are saying 'If only I'd started earlier!'.

Golf is not an old people's game: nothing could be further from the truth. Like any other sport, the earlier you start, the more chance you have of making rapid progress and being successful, especially if you play as a professional.

You often see children playing with cut-down adult clubs. Although this makes the club the right length for them, the weight and thickness of the grip mean the club is unbalanced. This makes it impossible to develop a good grip or swing, because the club simply doesn't feel right. If you do have a child who enjoys golf, there are plenty of inexpensive clubs designed especially for children, and when they have grown older you can always keep the clubs for their younger brother or sister or sell it to someone else.

Children don't need a whole set of clubs: three or four should be quite enough for a beginner.

Although it is never really too early to start playing golf, the ideal age is around 10 or 12. By this time, although they still have small hands, a child should be able to hold a club more or less correctly and be sufficiently strong to play a good backswing. It is a good idea to ask advice from a coach before you let your child take up golf; if they advise against it, the child could still take up putting.

If you are teaching a child, don't try to teach them how to play perfect strokes using perfect technique. Instead, insist that they play as naturally as possible, and focus on the four most important techniques: gripping the club, the address, pivoting and following through. The most important thing is that the child enjoys himself or herself and takes pleasure in playing, putting and hearing the ball drop into the hole.

At this kind of age, children are much better at learning by imitation, which is why it is a good idea that children act as caddies for the better players in the club and learn from their successes and mistakes.

Many golf clubs now accept teenagers and hold special group sessions for young people, which brings in the important element of peer rivalry. But there is also a lot to be said for giving your child the occasional individual lesson yourself so that you can keep a healthy parental eye on their progress and help them to concentrate on the game rather than simply trying to hit the ball as far as possible.

● Couples

1. Only one of you plays golf. In most situations, the woman will be the one who does not play, either because she stays at home looking after the children or because she prefers less male-dominated sports.

This can be a serious problem if the husband is away playing in competition at weekends. I also meet women who say that whenever they have people round to dinner the conversation always turns to golf, and if they're not golf players themselves, it's very hard to get interested. They see the rules and the technique as being far too complex to understand, and as a result golf can often place severe strains on a marriage.

2. Both of you play golf. At best, this can make for a very healthy relationship where you can spend the evening alone, or with other golfing couples, talking shop. But at worst, this situation can be just as problematic as one where only one of you plays golf. Because the man is often a better player than the woman because of his physical advantages, and because she is likely to have taken up golf later than he did, all too often the man suddenly discovers his hidden talents as a teacher. As a rule, spouses do not make good teachers, and again this situation can often end in acrimony.

3. Both of you play golf to a similar standard. The best example of this situation is Marie-Laure de Lorenzi-Taya, a French professional. Her husband, Roman, is an amateur with a handicap of 1 who plays for Spain. Marie-Laure had an outstanding amateur career before going professional in 1987. Since then she has put in some very fine performances, with her husband acting as both her coach and her caddie. Because he knows her playing style and its strengths and weaknesses like the back of his hand, he is also able to provide psychological support. They also have a small daughter whom they take out on the course with them as often as possible. So it is possible to have your cake and eat it!

● The caddie

A good caddie will play the role of friend, parent and confidant, but they are often also the first to come under fire if things go wrong. Even the world's top players need advice from a caddie when playing in competition: someone who knows both the player and the game inside out. Ideally, a player and their caddie should form a perfect partnership, with the player using their technique, skills and strategy and the caddie using his or her knowledge of the player and their strengths and weaknesses. The caddie also needs to know the course, be able to work out the distance between the ball and the pin down to the yard, know where the wind is blowing from and how hard, the size of each green, where the hole is, and how the course slopes.

Caddying is a highly skilled job, learned either from years of club experience or at the special schools which exist in Spain, the United States and elsewhere. It is very hard, very complex work; contrary to the common misconception, it does not simply involve replacing divots and keeping the golfer's clubs clean.

It is also a job that takes a great deal of patience and tolerance. If the player misses shots, the caddie is often the first person they vent their anger on. A caddie should be an endless source of encouragement and reassurance who gives the player the confidence to win and minimizes the number of mistakes he or she makes.

How Professionals Deal with Stress: a Survey

This survey was administered to 50 golf professionals in the form of a questionnaire. Only seven of them were women, but this reflects the limited number of women golf professionals in Europe.

The survey was intended to identify the psychological factors which affect professionals and keen amateur golfers. The questions examine general attitudes to golf, the psychological aspects that affect results in competition and, where the pros also worked as coaches, what methods they used.

Where the total comes to more than 100 per cent, it is because more than one answer was possible.

How do you deal with stress in the 24 hours before a match?
- Don't feel stressed: 42.5%
- Relaxation/sleep/
  medicines/music   32.5%
- Cinema/TV   15.0%
- Sex   10.0%
- Exercise, practice   10.0%

Does pre-match stress ever cause you physical problems, and if so, which?
- No 42.5%
- Yes 62.5 %

Insomnia	32.5%
Abnormally fast heartbeat	17.5%
Stomach problems	12.5%

Other symptoms mentioned were lumps in the throat and muscle cramps.

How do you deal with stress when you tee off?
- Arriving at the tee at the
  last minute   8.0%
- Visualizing the path of the
  ball and the target area   30.0%
- Deep breathing   30.0%
- Standing away from the
  crowd and practising
  strokes   22.0%
- Auto-suggestion (I'm the
  best, this is an easy
  shot etc.)   10.0%

Other methods mentioned were: thinking of the people I love, thinking of a funny situation to make me smile.

How do you deal with difficult parts of the course?
- Carefully (change club,
  half-shot, accept that I'm
  going to drop a stroke,
  etc.)   76.5%
- Take risks   32.5%

How do you deal with stress on the green?

- Don't feel stressed on the green — 17.5%
- Relax by thinking of technical aspects (grip, line of putt, nature of green etc.) — 32.5%
- Concentrate on target — 27.5%
- Listen to what my body is telling me (e.g. breathing) — 22.5%

What percentage of your performance do you think is down to psychology?

70% or more — 50.0%
40 to 70% — 30.0%
Less than 40% — 20.0%

Are you ever superstitious when you play golf?

- Yes — 52.5%
- No — 47.5%

Of those who said they were superstitious, 85 % said they always used the same method to replace the ball on the green before putting. The next most common form of superstition involved the colour of accessories such as the tee, the ball or the player's clothes. Other superstitions mentioned included:

- Always wear the same pullover, even in hot weather.
- Always take an even number of steps to reach the ball, especially on the green.

- Make sure my eyeshade is perfectly straight on my head and the stripes on my clothes are straight.
- Always walk onto the tee from the left.
- When I mark my ball on the green, always use the same coin, with the same side up and facing the same way.
- Never stay in an odd-numbered hotel room; always enter the hotel by the same door.

Do you have a more 'scientific' method for regaining your confidence?

During matches

- Use a different technique — 50.0%
- Adopt a different strategy — 42.5%
- Forget I'm playing golf, enjoy my surroundings, think of someone I love — 7.5%

Between matches

- Practice — 60.0%
- Relaxation techniques — 25.0%
- Hobbies, and other forms of escapism — 15.0%

Has golf ever been like a drug to you? Have you ever suffered from withdrawal symptoms?

- Yes — 60.0%
- No — 40.0%

How often do you dream about golf?

- Often — 25.0%
- Sometimes — 47.5%
- Never — 27.6%

Dreams about success (such as winning an Open, playing with famous people, flying round the course) were considerably outnumbered by nightmares. Some of the more common situations were:

- Arriving late for the start.
- Leading after the first round and not being able to find my car keys to get to the course on the second day.
- Not being able to play because the shaft of my club is too floppy.
- Not being able to get to the start because there is a locked door in the way.
- Not being able to see the hole.
- Teeing off from somewhere dangerous like the edge of a narrow balcony.
- The hole becoming an odd shape, such as an open mouth.

Do you ever take any form of medication to help you?

- Yes   25.0%
- No   75.0%

Are you more than usually careful about your diet?

- Yes   66.7%
- No   33.3%

Is sex good for your game?

- Yes, makes me more relaxed 40.0%
- Neither good nor bad   42.5%
- Bad, makes me tired   10.0%
- Bad, distracts me   7.5%

In your everyday life, are you more of a sensory or a visual person?

- Sensory   50.0%
- Visual   50.0%

When you play golf, do you tend to make more use of physical sensations or images?

- Sensations   76.5%
- Images   22.5%

Can you name any relaxation techniques?

- No   40.0%
- Yes   60.0%

(Meditation 55%, massage 35%, other relaxation techniques 10%)

Do you practise any of them?

- Yes   37.5%
- No   62.5%

What kind of attitude do you adopt towards a golf course?

- Friendly, try to win it
  over   50.0%
- Aggressive, try to
  dominate it   25.0%
- Respect it   25.0%

Bibliography

Adatto, Carl, M.D., 'On Play and the Psychopathology of Golf', *I.A.P.A.*, vol 12, 1964

Antonelli, Ferruccio, *Psicologia e Psicopatologia dello Sport*, E. Leonardo, Rome, 1963

Boon, Henry and Davron, Yves, *Relaxez-vous par la Sophrologie*, Editions Delarge, 1978

Bouet, Michel, *Sociologie du Sport*, Editions Universitaires, Paris 1968

Cei, Alberto, *Mental Training*, Luigi Pozzi, 1987

Chieger, Bob and Sullivan, Pat, *Golf Quotations*, Stanley Paul, 1987

Chimock, Frank, *How to Break 90 – Consistently*, J.B. Lippincott, 1976

Cook, Chuck and McCleery, Peter, *Tips from the Tour*, Golf Digest, 1986

Crandford, Peter G., *The Winning Touch in Golf*

Damiano Michel, *Strategie pour un Parcours de Golf*, Edition A.G.E., 1986

Diff, A. A., *Instant Golf Lessons*, Golf Digest, 1978

Gallwey, Timothy, *The Inner Game of Golf*, Pantheon Books, 1979

Garaïalde, Jean, *Golf*, Robert Laffont, 1988

Hogan, Charles, *Golf: Risultati Eccezionali in 5 giorni*, De Vecchi, Milan, 1987

Jacobson, Edmund, *The Modern Treatment of Tense Patients*, Chicago, 1926

Leadbetter, David, *The Golf Swing*, Collins Willow, 1990

Le Tellier, Philippe, Delanoe, Pierre and Lafaurie, Andre-Jean, *Golfantasmes* Albin Michel, 1986

Murphy, Michael, *Golf in the Kingdom*, Delta, New York, 1972

Nicklaus, Jack, *Golf my Way*, 1974

Nicklaus, Jack, *Playing Lessons*, Golf Digest, 1976

Rotella, Robert and Bunker, Linda, *Mind Mastery for Winning Golf*, Prentice Hall 1981

Schultz, J.H. *Le Training-autogene*, PUF, Paris, 1974

Norman, Thelwell, *Play it as it Lies*, Methuen, 1987

Toski, Bob and Flick, Jim, *How to Become a Complete Golfer*, Golf Digest, 1978

Toski, Bob and Aultman, Dick, *The Touch System for Better Golf*, Golf Digest, 1988

Wiren, Gary, *The New Golf Mind*, Simon & Schuster, 1978